Rita —
I don't know best
where this is best
at a Birthday Gift
a Post Nebr or Pre-Marr
Present. Consider it some of all
Three. Enjoy your trip,
and most of all
Congratulations !!

love
Fred

WORK
AND
LOVE
The Crucial Balance

Jay B. Rohrlich, M.D.

SUMMIT BOOKS
NEW YORK

Library of Congress Cataloging in Publication Data

Rohrlich, Jay B
Work and love.

Bibliography: p.
1. Work—Psychological aspects. 2. Love.
I. Title.
BF481.R63   158.7   80–14727
ISBN 0–671–40087–8

Acknowledgments

There are three people to whom I must extend special thanks for their help in turning my ideas and my writing into a book: Charlotte Sheedy, Paul Bresnick, and Jim Silberman. Carl Glick gave me great support and encouragement, not to mention his keen insights into the mind of Wall Street. Paul Prosky shared many profound personal reflections about his unique life role, and my wife, Marianne, taught me what being a mother truly entails. Michael Sacks was enormously helpful when I needed it most. And thanks also go to my son and daughter who provided me with the inspiration to bring this book to completion.

For my wife, Marianne

Contents

III:

WHY WE WORK

IV:

IMBALANCE

V:

THE CRUCIAL BALANCE

The essence of things escapes us, and will escape us always; we move among relations; the absolute is not in our province.
—Henri Bergson

Work was for him, in the nature of things, the most estimable attribute of life; when you came down to it, there was nothing else that was estimable. It was the principle by which one stood or fell, the Absolute of the time; it was, so to speak, its own justification. His regard for it was thus religious in its character, and, so far as he knew, unquestioning.
—Thomas Mann, *The Magic Mountain*

I love my work with a love that is frantic and perverted, as an ascetic loves the hair shirt that scratches his belly.
—Gustave Flaubert

Introduction

When I was about to complete my psychiatric training, and in the process of deciding where to open an office, an investment analyst friend of mine suggested, "Why don't you come to Wall Street?" Although he said it half in jest, the idea was intriguing. As a young person just establishing a career, the safer course would have been to locate myself in a more traditional area. I had a family to support, and if a Wall Street psychiatry practice was such a good idea, I thought someone else would have been there before me. To the best of my knowledge, nobody had.

For six years, I took the safer route and had an office in an uptown Manhattan residential neighborhood with a high concentration of practicing psychiatrists. But my friend's original suggestion continued to intrigue me. For one thing, many of the patients I was seeing happened to work in the Wall Street area. Either they took considerable time out of their workday to come to my office, have their sessions, and return to Lower Manhattan, or I had to see them at daybreak or late in the evening. It occurred to me that it would be easier for all of us if my office were near theirs.

There were other, more substantial reasons that made the idea of a Wall Street practice attractive. Wall Street was a community where half a million people worked, but virtually no one lived. Practicing there, where people in the legal, financial, and insurance industries would be coming to my office during their working hours fresh from work situations, would afford a direct entree into the dynamics of their work experience.

I had always been fascinated by how work and occupation influenced people's lives. In my own case, the decision to become a physician and a psychiatrist may have had as much or more to do with the kind of person I became than any other decision I have made in my life, or any other influence that affected my development. My sense of identity and the quality of my external life continue to be shaped and defined powerfully by my career. I often asked myself how the outlines of my life would have been altered if I had become, say, an English professor, and how my personality might possibly have differed.

In medical school, the decision to become a psychiatrist was as much influenced by my looking at the lives and personalities of people who were psychiatrists as by my interest in the stuff of a psychiatrist's work. And I still wonder whether the impersonal, unemotional quality of, say, a surgeon's personality implies that only certain kinds of people choose a field such as surgery, or whether these personality traits are the result of maintaining the mental state required to perform surgical procedures day in and day out.

The patients I was seeing from the financial and legal communities stimulated my curiosity about the role of work in life because so many of them seemed obsessed with their work and their careers. Perhaps "obsessed" is not the proper word, for it can connote abnormality and even pathology. In some cases of Wall Street lawyers and financial people who were involved with work to the virtual exclusion of all else, this connotation was apt. But in other cases it was not. For these people, work was something which aroused passion and deep devotion—they talked about it with great interest and insight, and their careers defined them and enriched their lives—but work did not "obsess" them. I became fascinated by the question of where we draw the line between enthusiastic *devotion* to work and *addiction* to work.

Many of my patients were troubled more by problems in their work environments than by those in their personal lives. People who were out of work for one reason or another went through emotional and personality changes as profound and disorganizing as others who were experiencing death, divorce, or other deep losses at home. Job and career decisions touched off enormous amounts of anxiety, and this was often the main reason that many people decided to seek therapeutic help. I was continually compelled to ponder the meaning of work in people's lives, and decided to study the entire issue more thoroughly.

It seemed to me that the work of my patients who were stockbrokers, traders, and investment bankers was a purer, more single-minded kind of work than that of those in other fields. The work done by a shoemaker or an artist is not simply an expression of aggressive, goal-directed energy; it involves materials and tangible products from which direct sensory enjoyment can be derived. No equivalent sensory experience is available or seems necessary to a stockbroker or a banker. Their primary work materials are numbers. A businessperson can take pleasure in a beautiful dress design or automobile that his or her company manufactures. In service professions such as medicine, even though a tangible or beautiful "product" may not be the goal of the work, there are opportunities for direct emotional involvement and pleasure. But in the "money" business, there is, for the most part, only financial profit and its rather single-minded pursuit. It seemed to me to be a pure kind of aggressive work, and for someone interested in studying the psychology of work, Wall Street appeared ideal.

Where else but on Wall Street can one hear, as I did from a famous and enormously successful corporate financier, that "paranoia is the key to high achievement in this business"? He explained, "The paranoiac is never distracted by kindness or generosity. He is always armed with a most adaptive delusion. He believes that everyone is out to get him. On Wall Street, he's right; and, in this community, he can function on the highest level. He is never secure, he never rests. The paranoid person is always working to be one step ahead of his enemies. He's the man I give my money to. Not the nice, well-adjusted guy."

Several years ago, I did move my office to Wall Street. My patients include many strongly work-oriented and successful people. They talk as much about their work as about their families, and through them I have been able to learn a great deal about the dynamics of work in the human personality. In addition, I have been a psychiatric consultant to large corporations in the Wall Street area. My consultations have focused primarily on troubled workers, managers, and executives whose problems have surfaced in the work setting. The opportunity to study all facets of the dynamics of work has been extraordinary.

An additional gratification from doing psychotherapy with highly work-oriented people lies in the fact that, in general, they are men and women who take themselves and their personal growth quite seriously. They are not content to view therapy merely as palliative support, and they work with characteristic discipline and determination to effect substantial personality change. For a psychiatrist, working with these people is enormously rewarding.

One of the most fundamental life problems that I have come across in my psychiatric practice, and in my own life, is the dilemma of finding the proper balance between work, family, and leisure. An extremely successful investment banker came to see me in deep depression after his fifteen-year-old son had attempted suicide. He felt that he was somehow at fault for his son's despair because he had worked so hard in his business, perhaps at his family's and particularly his son's expense. It was a poignant problem, and the dynamics were not at all clear. He was an ambitious and creative man who was passionately involved in his work. Was he "too involved"? Not only was there no simple answer, but I was aware that we had only the beginnings of a context in which to deal effectively with the question.

Other fascinating and important questions relating to work arise with my patients quite frequently. What is it about work that enables some people to be extremely successful in their careers but hopelessly ineffective and unhappy in their personal lives? And what about those who are kind and imaginative, but cannot be productive? How do we understand and interpret the increasing desire of young people to forego children in favor of career? What are the problems arising out of dual-career families? Is mothering a kind of work, like other jobs, or is it something different? Should mothering be supplemented with paid, career-oriented employment to foster optimal psychological development in women? What about men who choose to rear children while wives are the breadwinners?

The "crises" of midlife and retirement are basically problems related to the changes in the role of work at different phases in our lives. How do people in their forties handle the realization that there are limits to what they will achieve and accomplish in life? What is the relation between work achievement, identity, and sense of self? Thoughtful segments of the women's movement have developed the idea that occupation and self-worth are intimately related. Problems involving self-esteem are central to virtually every clinical case I deal with as a psychiatrist. There is no question that work and career have profound effects on the sense of self and personal value. Pride, satisfaction, glory, and fame are all work-related concepts. What do they mean? How do we understand them in terms of the overall personality?

Some of the most interesting people that I have known in my practice, and among my friends and colleagues, are those who seem never to stop working even when they are away from the job. They have led me to the conclusion that *working is not merely a state of employment, but a state of mind.* There are some people who are working even when they are playing. They are working when they are making love, or when they are on vacation. They have to be in control of themselves and their environments at all times. They seem unable to live for the moment. They think in black and white; numbers and measurement are central to their views of themselves and of the world. Mastery, accomplishment, and satisfaction, through the achievement of goals, are what their lives are about. Pleasure outside the realm of work is a bewildering and alien experience. If they are able to love, they seem to love only what they can create and control themselves. Compromise, emotionally, means surrender, and "the principle of the thing" is their favorite rationalization. Such work "addicts" have enabled me to study the process and meaning of work through a magnifying glass. In them, work is exaggerated, enlarged, abundantly visible.

To the best of my knowledge, no one has ever repudiated Freud's contention that the basic requirements of human existence are love and work. No one has ever told us, however, what this really means. What is love? What is work?

And what is leisure? Our current understanding of leisure is superficial and conceptualized only in negative terms. "Leisure time" is a concept which has had utility only since the industrial revolution, when work and workers had to be organized around very strict time boundaries. The need to synchronize the activities of large numbers of people in complex mechanical operations gave rise to the tyranny of the clock. Work was done in fixed-hour shifts. Trade unionism led to payment for time, not specific productivity. Leisure was defined simply as that time when you were not on the job.

In executive, professional, entrepreneurial, scholarly, and creative work, clear demarcations often do not apply between work time and leisure time. The clock does not necessarily begin our workday or send us home. And even at home, bulging attaché cases attest to the fact that this is not a nine-to-five world. In "higher-level" occupations, one's work may even be one's hobby.

The distinction between work and leisure becomes blurred in other ways as well. Business is often conducted in traditionally "leisure-oriented" settings. Executives make important deals in luxurious restaurants or on the fairways of golf courses. Many jobs provide opportunities for exciting travel which can nullify the desire for vacations. One resort advertises with the headline "Business and Birdies." The copy, extolling the virtues of their conference center, reads, "And when the day's business is done, all of our matchless recreational facilities are at your disposal: championship golf, tennis, swimming, health spa, riding, fishing, skeet, and more . . . plus 16,000 glorious mountain acres. Business and pleasure; at last the twain meet." For many men and women in these settings, moreover, there is ample opportunity for sexual liaisons which further obscure the work-leisure distinction.

There is no active verb in our language which is derived from the word "leisure." It is a static noun or an adjective ("leisure time," "leisure activity") which ignores the possibility of "leisuring" as an independent, active process. It is defined in one dictionary as "freedom provided by cessation of activities, engagement, or responsibilities." Such terms as "to relax" negatively describe an *absence* or *reduction* of muscle tension, subjective anxiety, or mental concentration. Even when we talk about "vacation," "retirement," or "free time," we imply the absence of work, not the presence of something else. "Doing nothing" is synonymous with leisure. The root of "vacation" is "vacate," "to cause to be empty or unoccupied." "Retire" comes from the French *retirer*, "to withdraw."

When we think of "leisure" as only the negative of work and not as a true opposite or as something positively defined in itself, we do not enhance our understanding of either process. In a survey conducted several years ago, a cross section of American executives were asked if they would continue working even if they inherited enough money to live comfortably without working. Eighty percent said they would continue to work. What is most fascinating about this information is that only 9 percent of these people said they would continue working because they enjoyed the work they were doing.* These statistics should be interpreted cautiously, but one factor that has to underlie them is the apparent inability to recognize leisuring as an alternative to working. In keeping with the current interest in adult-phase development, new terms like "leisuring" can be used to supplement such childhood-oriented words as "playing." Adults certainly do play, but they do more than that, and our vocabulary will be enriched if we can capture the precise complex quality of this aspect of "grown-up" psychology.

*Survey quoted in A. Hecksher and S. de Grazia, "Executive Leisure," *Harvard Business Review*, July–August 1959.

The essence of leisuring emerges from the same emotional source as loving. If we enlarge our understanding of the psychology of love we will better understand how to harmonize it with its companion process, work.

Since fulfillment in life is undoubtedly related to the quality of our love and our work, we can certainly profit from knowing what these concepts really signify in terms that are useful in our everyday lives. Our grasp of love and work can be more than descriptive. We can know something about their internal, psychic dimensions, not just their external, behavioral derivatives. Working and loving are states of mind. The quality of our lives depends on a healthy balance between them.

PART I

The Work Experience

1

Goals

The story of a friend of mine is a painful illustration of the importance of knowing what the role of work in our lives is all about.

He died of a sudden heart attack while on vacation with his wife in the Caribbean. He was a man of apparently robust health and limitless energy until that day when he lay on the warm beach looking into a cloudless sky. Chief of surgery at a major metropolitan hospital, he maintained a large private practice, commuted from a house in the suburbs, wrote and published extensively, and attended frequent professional meetings locally and throughout the country. He was rarely home before nine in the evening and began work at seven each morning, which necessitated his leaving his house by five-forty-five.

He enjoyed the two-and-a-half-hour daily commute because it enabled him to read and write on the train. He resented sleep as unproductive. His weekends were packed with home-based projects when he wasn't attending conferences or writing. He once told me that as Fridays approached each week, he would inevitably experience mounting tension if he had to anticipate forty-eight hours of unstructured time. This would be diminished if he had several projects to look forward to, such as building a tree house with the kids, rotating the tires on his two cars, or mowing his forty thousand square feet of Kentucky bluegrass lawn. As Sunday evening came, the heavy burden of weekend leisure began to lift, and by Monday morning, he admitted that he virtually sailed into his office or the operating room with a sense of thrill and challenge. He admitted that he made halfhearted complaints about how hard he worked, how badly he wanted to spend more free time with the family, and how he longed to travel with them, but he knew that he really could not.

In fact, he always had reasons for being unable to take more than a few days' vacation each year with the family. His wife became accustomed to spending most vacations waiting for her husband to extricate himself from some urgent problem which inevitably arose to destroy their plans. Or he would seem to "get sick" before or during the vacation. When he did get away, much of his time was spent on the telephone, or writing and reading important professional material.

The year he died was going to be different. He promised his wife, who was becoming quite depressed herself, and had given him a gentle ultimatum, that he was going to take a three-week vacation in the true sense of the word. After his death, many of his friends and family members agreed that his heart simply could not sustain such a driving, punishing work pattern.

The question, however, is: What really killed him? Was it the work, or was it the vacation? He was literally phobic about time he spent that had no fixed purpose, no defined end point or "product," and time that had no organization involving a regular sequence of skillful activities. Evenings at home, weekends, vacations, and thoughts of retirement were anguishing, disorienting experiences for him unless he was "meaningfully" occupied. Is it not possible that for him the enforced "relaxation" of the vacation proved to be lethal?

So many complex factors enter into the causes of illness that it would be foolish to suggest that only one variable caused my friend's untimely death. But his situation does raise some very important questions about work and leisure. Both can be defined in terms of external, behavioral, descriptive characteristics, but the critical dimensions of work and leisure are internal and intra-psychic. So far, these deeper dynamics have been inadequately studied.

In the past several years, the term "workaholic" has begun to appear frequently in popular and professional literature. The man who credits himself with inventing the term is Dr. Wayne Oates, a minister and professor of the psychology of religion. His book *Confessions of a Workaholic*, which appeared in 1971, provides many colorful descriptions of facets of work addictions. But like other discussions of this condition that have appeared since, Oates' book lacks a systematic analysis of the psychological process of working.*

Perhaps the fact that working is so much a part of our everyday experience is what accounts for this inattention. Unlike sex, working is an entirely nondiscretionary activity for most of us. We absolutely have to work to survive, certainly to survive with some security and comfort. We know that some people seem to work harder than others, but we do not have a framework within which to define normal and pathological work. When painters, musicians, athletes, or dancers spend virtually every waking hour perfecting their

---

*I have tried to avoid conventional scholarly footnotes, but this book and works by other writers and researchers that I mention, as well as a number of books and articles that are not mentioned but may be of interest to readers, are listed in the Bibliography at the end of the book.

skills and creating works and performances of exquisite beauty, they are thought of as passionately devoted artists and are much admired. If lawyers or businesspeople drive themselves with similar energy and discipline, they are often considered to be work addicts.

Most of the literature on work has been produced by sociologists and anthropologists whose sources of information, quite naturally, are observable group phenomena, not the inner mechanisms of the individual mind. Their information is derived from what is visible in behavior and what is reported on a conscious level. Prominent students of work such as C. Wright Mills, Fredrick Herzberg, Daniel Bell, and Daniel Yankelovich primarily describe *how* people work, but their disciplines do not really offer avenues to data which may explain *why* people work in the ways that they do. They do not provide us with a basis for exploring optimal balances between work and leisure.

For example, Yankelovich posits four dimensions or themes of the contemporary American work ethic: the good provider as the masculine ideal, the quest for independence, the desire for success, and the association of hard work with self-respect. Although these work-ethic themes are accurate in their general applicability to contemporary American culture, they do not come close to enabling us to understand what forces guided my work-addicted friend to his death on the beach. Such broad concepts as masculinity, independence, success, and self-respect are available for conscious rationalizing about determinants in working, but they only scratch the surface of potential understanding about individual motivation. They do not tell us what working is; they merely identify the values our culture has assigned to work. Sociological and anthropological perspectives approach work as a state of employment. It remains to be analyzed as a state of mind.

Most historical studies of work begin with the ancient Greeks, to whom work was simply a curse and the enemy of the independent spirit. The Greek word for work, *ponos*, also means "sorrow." It was music and contemplation that were set forth as ideals. Even Hesiod, who had no use for idleness and preached on the concept of work, did not endow it with any intrinsic value or dignity. Work was grudgingly accepted as a means to the ideal state, never as an end in itself.

The early Hebrews took the Greek view of work and extended it slightly. It was no longer a tragic necessity, meaningless in itself, but was explained as a penalty for sin and a means of reacquiring a lost spiritual dignity. Work was still painful drudgery, but it began to be endowed with a meaning that went beyond the simple practical necessity of the Greeks.

The early Christians, like the Hebrews, believed that work was punishment for original sin, but they modified that strictly negative doctrine with the notion of charity. Work became a means of helping needy brothers, but it still had no intrinsic value for the worker unless it resulted in charity. St. Thomas Aquinas brought about a major turning point in the attitude toward work when he based the ideal social order on a hierarchy of professions and trades, which he ranked according to their worth to the community. Work had value now. It was the fundamental legitimate basis for society.

It remained for the Protestant Reformation to lay the groundwork for modern conceptions of work. Martin Luther maintained that work was divine, a way of serving God, and that human energies could legitimately be turned to the material world. With Calvin, these ideas were extended and systematized. Work was the will of God. As a primary value to God, ceaseless toil *suffices* to please Him.

The current Western perspective on work abandons God as the focus of worship and reveres instead the concept of individual fulfillment. Work does not serve God so much as it serves the psychological development and enrichment of the individual. Self-actualization and self-realization are basic rallying cries. Defining our identities through achievement and creative accomplishment is a primary goal in our society. The joy of mastery is, in some ways, a modern equivalent of religious ecstasy. Freedom to achieve personal satisfaction through tangible work accomplishment is a basic credo in trade unionism, feminism, and other liberation movements. Some feminists have talked about the job as a human right. Underlying their position is a modification of the classical Cartesian notion: "I work, therefore I am."

Still, the modern dilemma about work is, as Max Weber put it: "Do we work to live or live to work?" For purposes of personal enrichment and self-realization, is work an end in itself? Or is it a means to the acquisition of more leisure time, the time when real fulfillment can occur? There is no easy way out of the dilemma, and class differences play a major part in the approaches to this question.

The nobility of work is paradoxically not really a working-class concept, but a middle-class one. Work addiction is a condition of people who don't *have* to work hard to survive. The person who feeds his or her family by having two full-time laboring jobs is not a work addict. He or she is hardly motivated by neurosis, but by sheer reality.

Psychoanalytic literature ought to be the place to look for answers to questions about the motivations for work and explanations of the fears and inhibitions connected with it, but there has been disappointingly little systematic attention paid to work by psychoanalysts. When Walter Neff researched his 1964 paper "Psychoanalytic Conceptions of the Meaning of Work," he found fewer than a dozen papers relating to work among the thousands in the body of psychoanalytic literature. In my own research for this book, I was able to turn up only a few more studies. Although Freud maintained in *Civilization and Its Discontents* that the "parents of human civilization" are work and love, he spoke of work simply as a "compulsion . . . created by external necessity." As a subject for psychoanalytic investigation, it did not hold very much interest for him. Incidental observations are made throughout his writings, but he never made a detailed analysis of the unconscious factors in work motivation. (In a very interesting early paper, David Reisman has discussed what he sees as Freud's unquestioning Victorian attitude toward work. For Freud, according to Reisman, work was a social necessity based on the need to survive. Precisely how work differed from love was never systematically explained by Freud.)

Karl Abraham, one of the pioneer psychoanalysts in Freud's circle, wrote a paper in 1918 entitled "Observations on Ferenczi's Paper on 'Sunday Neuroses' " clearly describing the defensive function of working. He emphasized how forbidden sexual drives and fantasies can be warded off "only through intense work" in some people, thereby preventing "the outbreak of serious neurotic phenomena." He described the process as follows:

"These people make violent efforts to find escape from the demands of their libido by overstraining themselves in their vocational activities, in their studies, or in the discharge of other duties. They get into the habit of doing an amount of work far beyond normal requirements. Work becomes indispensable to them, just as morphine does to the morphinomaniac; and the urgency of this need steadily increases. When a neuropath of this kind suffers an outbreak of a real neurosis, physicians and laymen alike are prone to give a specious etiology, namely 'overwork.' . . . [W]hen such a person is forced into inactivity by illness or accident, the outbreak of a neurosis, or the getting worse of an existing one, is not infrequently the consequence. In such cases, the popular tendency is to connect the neurosis etiologically with the illness, the accident, or whatever else may have occurred previously. But in many cases, it can be ascertained at once that the repressed libido has overpowered the patient during the period of his forced inactivity."

I would only add here that "forced inactivity" can be caused not only by illness or accident, but also by evenings, weekends, vacations, and retirement. Furthermore, it is not only the outbreak of neurosis that may be precipitated by this inactivity. Depressions, psychosomatic diseases, alcohol and drug addictions, and out-and-out psychoses are also common resultants.

Some of Abraham's insights are applicable to current popular concepts of stress, particularly "executive stress." It is a common deception, as Abraham points out, to attribute the physical or psychological distress experienced by people in "high-pressure jobs" solely to the grave responsibilities, time demands, and difficult decisions intrinsic to those particular jobs. I say "deception" because in most circles, students who both research and clinically treat "stress" often fail to explore fully the personality dynamics of an individual to explain why he or she was drawn to such a job in the first place, and, furthermore, why he or she is compelled to react with such "all-or-nothing" intensity to the content of the particular job. At best, it is disturbingly shortsighted to attribute the problem of stress solely to the particularly taxing dimensions of a job and to the worker's presumably passive reaction to it, rather than to the highly intense work needs of the person.

This observation is not, of course, to deny that psychic stress is a widespread phenomenon. It has been estimated that the effects of stress cost American industry $20 million to $50 million a year through diminished productivity, absenteeism, alcohol and drug abuse, early career termination, mental illness, and "industrial sabotage."* But, like obesity, psychic

---

*This admittedly vague and probably understated statistic was given in Michael Norman, "Executives Learn to 'Manage' Stress," *New York Times*, March 20, 1978.

stress is a symptom, or constellation of symptoms, consciously upsetting to the person, but nevertheless often brought on
by unconscious forces within him or her. To be sure, obesity,
like stress, leads to all sorts of psychological maladjustments
and physical hazards. But I know of no truly effective,
long-range program for weight reduction that does not deal
with the *meaning* of the individual's irresistible desire for food.
Dramatic short-term results by "diet doctors" often cycle into
a return to obesity, and I am afraid that "stress doctors" are
fast establishing a similar industry with biofeedback centers
and three-day relaxation retreats, where tense executives and
managers learn how to relax their muscles by lying on their
office floors in between appointments. We are dealing here
with people who are not simply passive victims of external
stressors, but are, rather, people who for the most part cannot
resist these selfsame stressors. They rationalize job demands
with survival-related fantasies: "If I do not master all that my
work entails, my days are numbered." These rationalizations
are expressed in terms of fears of demotions, firings, transfers,
failure to "make the deal," and profound disgrace. The often
panic-level emotions, however, imply a sense of doom on the
verge of personal annihilation if work intensity lets up and
control is relaxed. Clearly, the need for economic security
cannot be the sole explanation for these feelings about work.

Furthermore, to attribute this work compulsion only to the
need to protect oneself from forbidden sexual desires (as
Abraham does) may be appropriate for some people, but it
does not go far enough as a general theory. If work were *only*
defensive, how could we explain the fact that it is often so
emotionally stimulating? A defense "puts the lid" on feeling
and sensation. It does not serve a gratifying and expressive
function. But, as we all know, work can be directly gratifying, even thrilling. In fact, the excitement, say, of an
inordinately complex design problem for the architect, or the
sense of gripping challenge a schoolteacher feels in guiding a

retarded child to learn to read, can even replace, temporarily, the need and desire for sexual gratification. It would be rigid, unfair, and simply unimaginative to attribute the depth of these pleasures in intense work solely to a need to repress or channel conflicted sexual feelings away from their real object.

Work does a lot of things. We can derive a secure sense of being loved from the admiration and respect we generate from our work. The products of work define and affirm a feeling of self in concrete ways that no other life experiences can. We may discharge and channel anger and aggression from other conflicts when we "attack" or "wrestle with" our work projects. A thrilling sense of triumph over an adversary follows successful completion of a challenging work task. We punish ourselves and reduce guilty feelings by driving our minds and bodies with a merciless workload. Our normal fraternal drives may be gratified by the camaraderie we may enjoy in the workplace among our same-sex colleagues. Furthermore, work is a means of dealing with our feelings about death and the passage of time: our works have a permanence which defies loss and change. Work organizes, routinizes, and structures our lives. It allows for the appropriate outlet of competitive strivings. It keeps us sane.

Work is goal-directed activity. If one's mind is focused on the aggressive achievement of a defined end point, one is at work. The ability to conceptualize goals is uniquely human. Except in the most rudimentary and primitive way, lower animals are not equipped to think in terms of purposes, objectives, aspirations, and results. They do not work as we know it.

Our most distinguishable attribute as humans is the ability to condense experience into symbols. We name things. We have symbolic languages. Lower animals may have a vocal apparatus which enables them to communicate a sense of danger or some other immediate sensation or instruction, but they cannot name or label experience. They cannot abstract themselves conceptually from immediate experience into a past or a future, or into some other place. We need words for that.

A goal is a symbol, a verbal concept, an intellectual abstraction which represents a desired achievement at some future time. It is not a real perceptible thing until we reach it. When a porter says that his morning's goal is to empty all the wastebaskets on the floor, he is demonstrating his ability to create a mental representation of a future state. The process which will take him there we call "work." Only when he reaches his goal can he experience it with his senses. Then it is real. The wastebaskets are empty. He can see it with his eyes. Until then, the goal is merely a mentally constructed symbol for something to come.

By being able to conceptualize future events, and to abstract ourselves from immediate sensation, we are able not only to do work. We are also subject to another uniquely human experience: worry. Although we tend to anthropomorphize our pets, lower animals do not worry. They cannot think ahead, which is basic to the capacity to worry. They cannot plan. Worry, or anxiety, arises when an anticipated event, consciously or unconsciously conceived, is threatened.

Survival is our most precious and most easily threatened goal. We are the only animals who know that we will die. A cow lolling in the pasture does not know anything about life span. She cannot conceptualize future events, so she cannot worry about the avoidance of death. If a wild horse charges the cow, she will experience fear, but fear and anxiety are very different emotions. Fear results from an immediate threat to survival, easily perceived by the senses. Anxiety, on the other hand, emerges from our ability to play out a scenario of the future in our minds.

God's words to Adam, "In the sweat of thy face shalt thou eat bread," may have referred to much more than the perspiration caused by the physical labor required to provide food, clothing, and shelter. "Sweat" is a metaphor for anxiety, as such phrases like "in a cold sweat" and "sweating it out" illustrate. God was condemning Adam to a *lifelong susceptibility to anxiety*. Work, even the creation of civilizations, is an outgrowth of "sweat" over survival. Work has traditionally been defined as that activity designed to bring us to the goal of survival. But survival is only one among many goals which give rise to work. It is, without question, our most fundamental goal, and the prototypical work goal. But it does not necessarily define work. *Work is any activity designed primarily for the realization and achievement of a goal, no matter what that goal may be.*

Webster's Unabridged Dictionary calls work "physical or mental effort exerted to do or make something; purposeful activity; labor; toil." This definition taps into the aggressive and purposive dimensions of working. The President's Task Force on Work in America defined it from a sociological perspective: "[Work is] an activity that produces something of value for other people."

My definition of the mental state of work is the following: *Work is the skillful organization, manipulation, and control of the external and internal environments, to achieve a desired goal most efficiently and effectively.* This definition applies whether we are talking about the work of a bus driver, a corporate attorney, a mother, a tennis professional, a politician, an auto mechanic, a painter, a writer, or a student. It applies to work "on the job," and work in leisure time.

The first key word is "skillful." "Skill" is the outcome of goal-directed learning. It is represented by the acquisition of intellectual and technical operations whose application leads to predictably positive results. Once we are equipped with definitions, say, for a well-played tennis game or successful corporate-management goals, we can evaluate the skill of the tennis pro or the corporate manager. We do this in terms of how closely their skills enable them to realize established goals. Without defined, commonly accepted objectives, the concept of skill is meaningless.

Skill applies to all goal-directed work. There is no such thing as "unskilled labor" or "unskilled work." If something can be called work, it must involve some skill or competence, however simple. The competence to achieve goals, any goals, even if they involve the simple objectives, say, of a restaurant doorman, always requires some skills. There are systematic ways to open a restaurant door properly, to greet customers, hail taxis, carry packages, and protect patrons. These are skills. They may be of a different order of complexity than the skills, say, of a nuclear physicist, but they are skills nevertheless. Skill defines the domain of work.

"Organization, manipulation, and control" refer to the operation of the analytic attitude and the aggressive instinct in all forms of working. No matter what the task, the worker must approach it by "breaking it down" into manageable blocks. This process is so automatic that we are usually unaware of its complex sequences even when we are performing them. In this sense, the process is something like walking, which requires the exquisite coordination of many neurological and muscular functions. The first step in the analytic approach to a problem, once the goal is established, is a naming or labeling of tools and materials. We screen out the extraneous and identify that which will lead to our goal. A painter must identify and accumulate what he or she needs to make a picture, and a manufacturer must do the same in embarking on a marketing program.

These tools and materials are organized on a desktop or in symbolic form in words listed in sequence on a page. Outlines represent the organization and manipulation of materials. Further manipulation occurs with the sequencing and scheduling of operations, each step designed with the goal clearly in mind. Scheduling involves the imposition of time constraints in structuring the goal-directed process. Strategies are developed. This all may be accomplished as symbolic, conceptual manipulation before any actual technical operation occurs. By symbolic, I simply mean the representation of the entire process in written or spoken word symbols. This ability to condense (or manipulate) our experience into verbal symbols clearly enables us to conceptualize and play out the future before we actually get there. It is the basis of planning ahead.

Technical manipulation of our materials implies their transformation by the worker. They are altered from one form to another, as the worker is oriented by an ever-present light beam emanating from the goal. An accountant takes raw data from canceled checks and petty cash vouchers and enters them, in new form, on a ledger sheet. A dancer puts the *demi-plié, battement tendu, glissade,* and *pas de chat* together into a unified performance sequence. Perfecting these new forms means imposing greater and greater degrees of control over them in accordance with proven methods and defined objectives. The aggressive nature of this entire process should be clear. We react to our materials as if they were adversaries to be subdued and dominated—not destroyed, but mastered. That is the essence of creative work.

The question arises whether this definition of work applies to all levels of workers, or simply to those who are involved in the interesting, challenging occupations which characterize the upper classes of our society. Does the person who operates a push-button elevator for eight hours a day truly organize, manipulate, and control his environment to achieve specific goals?

This question is related to the larger issue of the distinction between work as paid employment and work as a state of mind. Not all employment feels like work, or even can legitimately be called work, as many people with menial, repetitive, mindless, low-skill jobs will confirm. Because you're on a job, you are not necessarily working. The psychological definition of work which I have set forth refers to an *ideal mental state* that is not necessarily related to gainful employment, and it is against this ideal definition that we can measure the quality of our working lives.

I have described the manner in which the worker ideally applies his or her skills to organize, manipulate, and control the "external environment," the world of tools and materials. The worker does this as well to his "internal environment," his mind and body. The most dramatic example of internal manipulation and control is the process of *concentration*.

The dictionary defines "to concentrate" as "to bring or draw to a common center or point of union; focus." A convex lens "concentrates" the diffuse rays of the sun into a single burning point. "Concentric" circles telescope down to a point. When a worker concentrates, he or she overpowers diffuse mental activity to bring it to focus on a single objective, a narrowing rather than an expanding of mental perspective. Concentration implies a separation from, rather than a connection to, everything and everybody in the worker's immediate environment, except insofar as they relate to the specific task and objective. For some work-phobic people, this is a frightening experience because of the intense separation and isolation it requires. Fantasy and emotion are also excluded because they distract us from attention to our goal. Concentration is an aggressive act, performed on our own minds.

Interestingly, concentration may function as a form of anesthesia or narcotic. When a woman in labor concentrates on specific breathing patterns, she is able to anesthetize herself to the pain of uterine contractions. When a jogger concentrates on running ten miles in under fifty minutes, this intense focus on a discrete goal enables him to abolish his anxiety over troubles at the office or tensions at home with his family. Biofeedback and transcendental meditation are also based on concentration. Many people refer to simple, uncomplicated, goal-oriented tasks as their form of "therapy." *The New York Times* once featured an article about the fact that many people were taking music lessons instead of seeing psychiatrists. For them, concentrating on perfecting the F-sharp minor scale on the piano led to a liberating suspension of tension and anxiety and the eradication of distressing fantasies.* These people were focusing on simple, discrete, well-defined goals, and in doing so they were anesthetizing themselves against psychic pain. The ability to concentrate is, in fact, the basis of one's susceptibility to hypnosis. It is also the basis of successful work. Because it can function to protect us from anxiety and other painful feelings, it is easy to see how work is narcotizing and can become addictive. One can indeed "get high" on work.

Manipulation of the internal environment in the work process relates, of course, to the body as well as the mind. The tennis professional must subject all the muscles in his or her body to intense, aggressive control. The typist and the writer must do the same with the muscles in their hands and their buttocks. They must sit still for hours and hours. This is *discipline*.

Mental concentration, or the aggressive harnessing of all cerebral activity on the goal of a task, gives rise to what C. Wright Mills has called the *ulterior* quality of work. When we are concentrating on our goal and on the methods designed to take us there, we cannot permit ourselves to be distracted by fascination with or enjoyment of the materials immediately at hand. We must always be "getting on with it" or "getting to the point." Much of our attention needs to be focused beyond the immediate moment to the "future" goal. We must abstract

*Anna Quindlan, "Instead of Therapy, It's Music Lessons," *New York Times*, March 3, 1978.

ourselves from the present, while simultaneously attending to it.

Work is *productive* activity. It always leads to a product, a tangible creation like a book, a painting, or a pair of shoes, or a symbolic product like the sale of a block of stock memorialized in *The Wall Street Journal* or a tribute from a grateful patient. When people talk about "doing" something, they are really talking about "making" something. In French, *faire* means both "to do" and "to make." "Doing" something implies goal-directedness. Our work behavior points to a defined result, purpose, goal, or objective.

Because work is productive activity, it is always *linear*. A straight line is defined in plane geometry as that which represents the shortest distance between two points. The two points in the linear work situation are the worker and the product, the goal. The unidirectional movement between them we call work. A zigzag course to a stated goal, full of side trips to take in scenery, is inefficient and undermines effectiveness. Aggressive pruning of peripheral activity strengthens the linear growth of the central trunk. In the definition of work, achievement of a desired result is accomplished "efficiently." "Efficiency" implies linearity, a situation in which extraneous, non-goal-directed experience must be repudiated.

Knowing what is extraneous and inefficient requires the exercise of judgment and discretion. Decisions must be made, usually unconsciously, at all points along the path to an objective, to maintain its linear efficiency. Psychoanalyst Elliott Jaques emphasizes this discretionary dimension of the work process and distinguishes the different levels of work on the basis of the degree of discretion and judgment required in various roles.*

*In *Glacier Project Papers*, p. 164, Jaques defines "psychological work" as "the exercise of discretion within prescribed limits in order to reach an objective."

When we talk about our lives "having direction," we usually are referring to the establishment of long-range work goals which we efficiently pursue. If we're running after something, we go in a straight line. People whose lives are totally work-oriented, who are exclusively linear, are thought of as one-dimensional, as a straight line is one-dimensional. They have direction, but apparently nothing more.

One extremely important attribute of goals is that they help to define the identity of the person who pursues and achieves them. The work product is symbolic. It is a tangible, discrete, precisely defined extension of a person. As the German existentialist Martin Heidegger said, "You are your projects." In the same vein, one of my patients eloquently and simply concluded, "You are what you do." For most of us, identity is largely a function of successful, productive achievement. Work is *self*-centered in the purest sense, because the work product defines the self more objectively and concretely than any other aspect of our experience. A person who cannot point to his or her achievement does not feel like a full person. Subjective experience is too diffuse for self-definition. To say "I feel it" is not as definitive as to say "I did it." Nothing else with which we associate our selves can give us the sense of objective identity that work can. Work situations in which people do not derive a feeling of personal responsibility for the outcome destroy the worker's spirit. When we can say "I did it," we are enjoying the ultimate in self-definition. People who rely on saying "I have it" or "I belong to it" for their sense of self are lacking a critical dimension of personal identity. They are not creating new forms; they are merely joining old ones, or someone else's.

I have defined work as the *skillful organization, manipulation, and control of the external and internal environments, to achieve a desired result most efficiently and effectively.* The important word which we have so far not addressed is "effective." The more "effective" work is, the closer it comes to realizing a preconceptualized goal. It is the aggressive control and power over materials that is the key to "effectiveness." "Perfection," "greatness," "mastery," and "excellence" revolve around the instinct of aggression. Aggression is an all too often misunderstood instinct, assumed to be synonymous with rage and hostility. On the contrary, anger and hostility result from the *ineffective* exercise of aggression. People who fear and suppress their aggressive drives are usually unsuccessful in work.

2

Aggression

When people talk about work—artists, businesspeople, professionals, etc.—their language is laced with the following sorts of expressions:

— "I am about to *tackle* a new project in the marketing area."
— "I feel the need to *grapple* with new materials, maybe work in marble."
— "We *wrestled* all night over the timing of a new common stock offering."
— "I like work I can *sink my teeth into*."
— "I want that new salesman to have more *punch*."
— "With my camera, I feel like a big-game hunter *bagging* a perfect specimen. The satisfaction is immense."
— "We made a *killing* in last year's market."
— "The audience really responded to me. *I knocked 'em dead.*"

In his essay "The Sanity of True Genius," Charles Lamb said of "the true poet": "He is not possessed by his subject, but has *dominion* over it." We often talk of great artists "capturing" the essence of a beautiful scene. Monet is quoted by his friend Durand-Ruel as saying, "The countryside is superb, but so far I haven't been able to *take advantage of it*."*

The key words here, such as "master," "dominate," "capture," and "take advantage of," could just as well be describing a military battle as the creation of art. They convey the basic aggressive urge which underlies all work. Our need to struggle in our attempts to control our environments, to organize and master materials so that we can overcome our insecurity about survival, gives rise to our need to work. A personal work achievement, whether it is a new art form or a new business market, is a tangible sign of an individual's ability to foster his or her own survival. Remnants of early infantile helplessness are always present in our unconscious minds, and our drive to work is in part an effort to compensate for this anxiety. The aggressive drive catalyzes the development of language and the intellect, and the monuments of human civilization are a testimony to the free expression of creative aggression.

"Organization," "manipulation," and "control" epitomize aggression. They suggest an adversarial relationship to materials, even to our own mind and body. We are *doing* something to another object when we work, engaging ourselves in a process that is antagonistic and change-oriented. We are actively transforming materials; and deliberately changing something from one form to another is an aggressive act. *When the need to change materials has a constructive, creative goal, we call it work. When the desired change is destructive, we call it rage.*

The aggression we summon to engage in work also functions to master our own natural tendencies as workers. Concentration, as we have seen, is an aggressive overpowering of naturally chaotic or diffuse mental activity to bring it to

*Wildenstein, *Monet's Years at Giverny.*

focus on a single goal. Self-discipline, undoubtedly an essential element in effective work, represents a single-minded domination of natural physical and mental inclinations, a harnessing and controlling of muscle and mind.

Aggression and sex are the two innate, unlearned psychic drives in humans. They form the foundation of all behavior. We find or create outlets for the discharge and expression of these drives, and the outlets we develop define and color our lives.

Aggression is a catalyst for change, and naturally evolves into goal-directed activity. Seeking changes implies the ability to foresee that which is not yet available to the senses. Freud emphasized death and destruction in aggression. Post-Freudian thinkers have modified this negative view and focus more directly on constructive aggression.* But they agree in one major respect. *Aggression always involves change in an external object*. It is a drive whose aim is some *transformation* of a present state or some enforced maintenance of a present state against a natural inclination to change. Death, destruction, or construction all represent a manipulation of matter toward some goal. Hostile aggression, which is more primitive, certainly, than creative aggression, focuses on negative change: a punch in the mouth or a bomb in a bus are hostile, since their goal is to impair or take away life. *Aggression whose objective is to change the present to enhance or create future life is called work.* The more determined, the more aggressive, we are in achieving our goals, the more effective our work will be.

The need for mastery catalyzes the development of the intellect, which carves up and reduces experience to categories and verbal symbols. The intellect organizes and manipulates these symbols into meaningful language. Language enables us to abstract ourselves away from what our senses

*For example, see the articles by K. Menninger and by S.R. Slavson listed in the Bibliography.

perceive. In this way, it enables us to master not only our immediate environments, but those which are separated from us in time and space.

For those in whom the aggressive instinct predominates, there is always a *purpose* to the present; it cannot be experienced without the need to *do something* with it, to control it, change it, command it, or point it in the direction of some objective. The person who cannot permit himself to be immersed in the present through his senses, who must attempt to "capture" the beauty of a brilliant sunset in a photograph or poem rather than enjoy the inner glow of a momentary union with it, who must always be thinking *ahead*, who must always put his perceptions into words, who seems obsessed with constructive change and mastery, is a slave to the aggressive drive.

When we say that we are going to "do a *job*" on someone, going to "*work* someone over," or "give someone the *business*," we can appreciate how our language equates "work," "job," and "business" with domination, control, and power. But aggression, by controlling or dominating, does not necessarily destroy the object. It *transforms* the object. It is a constructive, creative, and adaptive drive, the fundamental aim of which is to foster the survival, preservation, and enrichment of our selves and our communities.

From this perspective, we can understand how aggression is not expressed simply in, say, the tough, shrill marching orders of a marine drill sergeant, but functions as well in the delicate, precise work of a watchmaker, or in the gracious but effective negotiations of an international diplomat. All are mastery experiences. Hostility and destructive rage arise only when aggression is thwarted, frustrated, and rendered ineffective. Then we get angry and want to inflict hurt.

Aggressiveness can also be a sign of love and caring. The father who vigorously grabs the arm of his son who is about to inject himself with heroin is showing his concern through an aggressive act. Being aggressively critical and forthright with a friend may sometimes be more loving than being passive and conciliatory about something we may disagree with or disapprove of.

Satisfaction is the emotion associated with the achievement of mastery. The dissatisfied infant is not able to "master" his mother's appearance and disappearance with his magical cry. Dissatisfaction turns to rage. Ineffective mastery in adulthood, a sense of failure, is what leads to anger, as illustrated in the following vignette about Monet, from Wildenstein's biography: "Monet could occasionally throw terrible tantrums. The reasons were almost always the same: a *failed* painting, a *recalcitrant* motif, a change in the weather that *forced* him to abandon a canvas for a time." (Italics added.)

This glimpse of Monet at work tells us about the adversary nature of work as well as about the genesis of temper. A motif is "recalcitrant." The weather "forces" him to abandon a canvas. Nature, in all its aspects, is here experienced as an adversary—something, although loved and admired, which is to be mastered, dominated, and transformed into a "work" of art. When Monet fails to "capture" what he wants of nature in his painting, he becomes enraged.

All forms of working are rooted in the aggressive attitude of "being against." Consider the noun "master." The same word describes the owner of a slave, the conductor of a symphony orchestra ("maestro"), and a group of legendary painters in the classic tradition ("the old masters"). We speak of "masterpieces" to describe works of outstanding accomplishment. The aggressive manipulation of emotional and visual material characterizes the work of a masterful artist.

Exploitation of environment, people, and objects underlies all work. "Exploit" means "to utilize, especially for profit; to use selfishly for one's own ends." Good businesspeople will not hesitate to agree that this is precisely their purpose. They may desire that their business products benefit other people, but the pursuit of personal profit has to be primary in their minds. A sensuous immersion in the materials of their work, however, is usually alien to the businessperson's objectives, as we have seen. It is a distraction, a pull toward the pleasures of the moment that contradicts the necessity for ulteriorization.

A poet also "exploits" the environment, but this exploitation is far more softened by the sexual drive than in the world of business. The poet organizes and manipulates materials, "works over" word sounds, visual images, cadences, emotionally charged concepts, syntax, and levels of semantic meaning. The personal "profit" involves the creation of a product, a fixed and desired result which delivers intense emotional rewards, personal enrichment, and self-definition to the creator. This aggressive dimension of the poet's work, however, is unlike the businessperson's because it is modified by a love for the materials which are being manipulated into a poetic creation.

Of course, businesspeople may see their work as being "for" their families or for the good of various others, and not simply for personal profit. Surely, money earned through aggressive work does enhance the quality of life for one's self and one's family. But this notion of work as a means toward love is quite a separate issue from the intrinsic aggressive nature of work itself.

3

Boundaries

In addition to its goal-directed and aggressive aspects, work can also be looked at as "structured" or "bounded" activity. Whether the ironic proposition in Robert Frost's "Mending Wall" that "good fences make good neighbors" is true or not, it is a fact that all people experience a need for order and definition in their lives. Structure requires walls, fences, and dividing lines. Boundaries orient us to the world. They provide "meaning." When we define something, we enclose it in a category. We put it within an orderly frame.

Work is the most visibly defined and bounded arena of our lives. Work goals establish a structure for our experience. Once a goal is conceptualized, and the efficient, linear realization of that goal is our desire, we are within a structure. We have a specific direction. We apply defined skills, established methods, techniques, and procedures to reach our goal. Time provides precise boundaries to our work activity. There are schedules and deadlines which harness and outline our endeavor.

What is relevant in the world of work can be put into words

and numbers. The more precise the categorization of something, the more useful it is in the working mode. Work is "meaningful" because it involves learning that is most accessible to factual definition. As a psychiatrist, I learn that when a patient begins to have hallucinations, it "means" that the patient is becoming psychotic. When a stockbroker sees a run of profit-taking in a particular security, that "means" that the price of that stock will begin to fall. When a potato farmer tells us that it's going to be a long, hard winter, that "means" that spring planting will be late, and crops will be delayed. When a trial attorney in cross-examination exposes contradictions in a witness' testimony, that "means" that he is gaining points for his client's cause. When an artist applies a line of green paint to the corner of a canvas, that stroke "means" an enhancement of the harmony of composition.

Each task in the farmer's repertoire has a specific set of rules, a precise framework of systematic procedures and definitions, governed by continuous attention to a desired end result. The farming task involves clearly bounded or defined techniques. Seed potatoes are cut in quarters, each with one or two eyes in it, planted in May in straight rows, twelve inches apart, in soil fertilized with nitrogen, potash, and phosphorus. The plants are harvested 120 days later, etc. Essential to being a successful farmer, or a successful worker in general, is the ability to master these kinds of facts and strategies, and to feel at home with technical data, methods, procedures, and clearly enunciated goals.

If definition in work is ambiguous, work breaks down. One woman told me of a situation in her company in which, for a variety of complex reasons, she one day found herself supervising a person who was earning $500 more per year than she was. It was an impossible situation for both parties, and it exploded before any productive work could be accomplished. Another, quite amusing example of this need for precise clarity of definition in work is contained in the story of

the Congressional clerk who was instructed to write: "All
foreign fruit-plants are free from duty." Instead, he wrote:
"All foreign fruit, plants are free from duty." It cost the U.S.
government two million dollars before a new session of
Congress could rectify the error. There is no aspect of our
personal lives where ambiguity of definition—in this case, a
comma instead of a hyphen—can have such far-reaching
consequences.

In the world of work, people themselves actually become
tools and materials in the goal-directed processes of work.
They are defined by roles, titles, earning levels, and technical
skills. They are "organized, manipulated, and controlled"
from within and without to create products and reach
objectives efficiently and effectively. This is not necessarily a
dehumanizing process. In proper doses, it imparts order and
meaning to our environments and to our selves. When it
becomes extreme, when people are carelessly stereotyped or
when they are manipulated in ways which may smother their
natural energies, work can indeed be repressive.

Human beings have the unique ability to reduce the chaos
of perceptual experience through the creation of symbols.
Our senses are bombarded continuously by billions upon
billions of stimuli from within our bodies, and from the
external environment. Our brains are equipped to simplify
this potential chaos, to organize, manipulate, and control it,
through the imposition of symbols. The most common
symbols that we use are words and numbers. And the world
where words and numbers have greatest application is the
world of work.

Developmental psychologists, such as Jean Piaget, Heinz
Werner, and Bernard Kaplan, have documented the growing
child's ability to "make sense" of the world around him by
organizing and condensing his perceptions into symbolic
categories. A word is an artificially constructed category, a

symbolic label, behind which stands a complex mass of information. The simple statement "That is a good job" is an example of how we reduce an infinitely complicated amount of data about a task and its many facets into five symbols called words. Without this ability to assign labels to our perceptual experience, we could not hope to put our conscious lives into any meaningful order.

Work is the primary source of life's labels. Its boundaries and categories not only orient us to the external world, but enable us to "know" ourselves as well. Self-definition implies the ability to feel contained within precise outlines. "I am a doctor. I am a cardiovascular surgeon. I am a surgeon specializing in coronary-artery bypass procedures." The more descriptive we can be about ourselves, and the more precisely defined the verbal categories we feel we belong in, the greater is our sense of self-definition.

The mathematician and scientist Jacob Bronowski said that the content of an hour lecture could probably be put into six sentences. The same can be said about the "content" of a person. Any person can be described in just a few phrases. But the more global the sentences, the more ambiguous they become. "Most of human sentences," said Bronowski, "are in fact aimed at getting rid of the ambiguity which was unfortunately left trailing in the last sentence." This applies to our sense of self-definition. The more sentences we can utter about ourselves—the more boxes we put ourselves in—the more we reduce our sense of *personal* ambiguity. The more detailed the "character study" we can make on ourselves, the greater is our sense of self.

The French philosopher Henri Bergson said, "The essence of things escapes us and will escape us always; we move among relations; the absolute is not in our province." He was maintaining that we operate in life without absolute standards and meanings. We do not know *why* we live or *what* we are. We only know that we are living, and we organize and shape our lives according to conventions which establish "relations" with one another. We are always "drawing lines." We make arbitrary distinctions between what's good or bad for us, what's too big or too small, or what's affordable or too expensive. There are no absolutes here. We draw our own lines, and the lines we draw define us as people.

A "weak person" has trouble drawing lines to establish defined and consistent tastes, preferences, beliefs, values, and opinions. Or he may draw arbitrary and capricious lines to give the illusion of strength and firmness. An adolescent, whose identity is in the process of forming, may feel intact and bounded only if he senses the uniform *dis*approval of all people around him. A stubborn person draws lines only when it is late in a situation, whereas a strong person knows his or her limits, and draws them clearly from the beginning.

In our civilization, the truth of the statement "You are what you do" is indisputable. We are known by others, and know and define ourselves, primarily by what projects we devise, by what products we create, and by the occupations which represent these productive pursuits. One may try to answer the question "Who am I?" with information other than that represented by our "works": "I am a person who smells flowers"; "I am angry feelings"; "I am running and hopping." But because personal identity, the sense of "I am," refers to the feeling of being a discrete, bounded, unique, recognizable unity—*a self*—this is most clearly derived from tangible symbolic extensions of the self: *our works*. In terms of time spent, it may be more accurate to say "I am angry feelings" than "I am a judge." But "angry feelings" do not draw lines around a person as visibly as an occupation does.

Nothing is so uniquely personal, so active a representation of an individual, as his or her skills and works. There are many kinds of self symbols: feelings, interests, loves, memories, opinions, tastes, clothing styles, national heritages, religions, material possessions, memberships, language accents, etc. But to give uniqueness to an individual, one relies most fully on one's own "piece of work." That piece of work may be a typed letter, a completed delivery route, or a best-selling book. The ability to say "I did it," whether one's impulse is based on contributing to the well-being of a new socialist society or to the health and comfort of self and family, gives us the ultimate in self-definition. All other associations to ourselves, even what we love or are interested in, are more passive expressions of self than what we do.

Women who turn away from mothering and homemaking to paying jobs, even relatively menial ones, are turning away from a form of experience whose "products" are in too great a state of flux and not sufficiently identified as one's own definitive creation to yield a specific sense of self. A teenage child or a gourmet meal is not the static, clearly bounded symbol of self that a set of balanced books or a courtroom victory is. It is a sad fact, although one which is changing, that wives who are homemakers often maintain a stable identity only through an association with the works of their husbands.

There is clearly a graded distinction between work, job, and occupation in terms of the degree of self-definition each confers. "Work" is a general term describing a goal-oriented, aggressive, structured state of mind. "Job" refers to an "applied" work situation, but if the job does not imply a particular occupation, self-definition is wanting. Some people go from job to job, from industry to industry to industry, at low-level or even high-level positions, to make a living. They cannot rely on their "works" to provide them with self-definition because nothing consistent is built, nothing grows and develops out of their work which identifies them tangibly in terms of occupation. One patient complained that he felt "scattered" as a human being because of his varied and disconnected careers. This, of course, is more pronounced in the lower socioeconomic levels, and is one of the reasons why the "work ethic" is primarily a middle-class concept. Only at higher levels can a worker identify himself with his product and truly sense its personal consistency and uniqueness.

A judge holds court in a certain manner, hands down decisions, writes opinions, and is known by these opinions to be a maker of mediocre or landmark decisions. His or her identity is largely formed as a composite of these and other works. They are held together by the concept of his or her occupation: jurist. Feelings, fantasies, and bodily sensations, although very much parts of a person's being, do not establish identity as concretely and visibly as do works. And a friendly, imaginative, unproductive person is less valued in our culture than an unfriendly, boring, but very productive person.

Psychiatrists talk of "ego boundaries" when referring to an intact sense of personal identity.* Schizophrenia is an illness characterized by defective ego boundaries. People who suffer with it are often confused about the limits and the outlines of their identities. A seriously disturbed schizophrenic person can sometimes look at his own hand or face in the mirror and feel that it is not his hand or that it is someone else's face. There is no sense of integrity to the self, no feeling of personal intactness and continuity. A less disordered person may reveal his boundary diffusion not in terms of his body, but in terms of ideas or thoughts. He may feel that his thoughts are either borrowed or easily stolen, and not a definite part of his or her self.

One patient of mine remarked that when he was in a group and someone told a joke, he could always detect a split-second lag period between the time everyone else laughed and when

---

*The foundation of this concept was provided by Paul Federn. The introduction to his *Ego Psychology and the Psychoses*, by Edoardo Weiss, is especially helpful in explaining Federn's formulations regarding ego boundaries.

he did. He was never sure if his laughter was truly "his," or if he was merely merging with the group. A boundary deficiency is exemplified in this confusion. When his perplexity became pervasive and applied to all of his personal interactions, this patient became psychotic. His speech would be incoherent and jumbled, he would wander aimlessly through the streets, and he could not organize his perceptions into any recognizable conceptual frameworks. He became overwhelmed by external and internal sensations which he could not categorize and label. One typically psychotic tactic which he used for reducing the chaos in his mind was holding onto some peculiar, highly personalized article of clothing, or carrying some idiosyncratic object with him at all times. The familiar "crazy" person walking the streets with a shopping bag full of strange letters and old newspapers is trying, in a primitive way, to accumulate external symbols through which to identify himself. Fixed, single-minded delusions ("I am Jesus Christ," or "The CIA is after me") which obsess the psychotic person are another extreme way of imposing order on a chaotic mind.

It is no accident that the treatment of schizophrenia often involves "occupational" approaches. Patients are trained to learn specific skills and to create worthwhile products, truer and more deeply meaningful symbols of self than some idiosyncratic keepsake. Symbols, in this case personal works, "stand for" the self, and define it in a tangible, communicable, and active form. In this sense, our novels, paintings, realestate deals, balanced books, and judicial opinions are synonymous with our "selves."

Recommending a vacation to a person in the throes of a schizophrenic psychosis is the last thing one would want to do. Leisure activities, which involve the diffusion of boundaries and an immersion in sensation, terrify the schizophrenic. Personal intimacy of any sort can throw him into panic and psychotic confusion. It is for this reason that a highly structured, perhaps exaggeratedly defined environment is necessary in the treatment of this condition. A few years ago, on a mental-hospital ward where I was working, nurses went from wearing traditional white uniforms to everyday street dress in an administrative experiment. The result was catastrophic. The patients were deprived of an orienting, clearly defined landmark, and were thrown into unbearable confusion. They could not easily tell nurses from patients. But the staff enjoyed their liberation from the strictures of the uniform, and settled on compromising by adding nametags. In a larger sense, the patients might have been reacting to exactly what contributed to their conditions in the first place: the contradiction of facts they knew very well—in this case, the cosmetic contradiction of the status and authority differences between them and the staff.

It is a common misconception that "overwork" can cause mental breakdowns. For example, one author, describing the psychotic collapse of Zelda Fitzgerald (wife of novelist F. Scott Fitzgerald), ascribed her having been placed in a psychiatric sanatorium to her compulsive, all-consuming ballet dancing. On the contrary, her overwork was undoubtedly an effort to stem the tide of a psychotic process which was already beginning. In this breakdown of the personality, the normal boundaries around the self begin to weaken and come apart, and work becomes a compulsive attempt to reassert them. In Zelda Fitzgerald's case, it was "ballet work." Her underlying emotions were of such power, though, that they could not be managed "occupationally" and the eventual breakdown occurred. The "overwork" and the mental collapse were only temporally, and not causally, related.

One patient shed light on this "therapeutic" dimension of work by using the example of a tennis court to explain his passion for his job: "If you're hitting a ball back and forth with another person, all you have are the sensations of your body, the impact of the ball, movement, the air around you, and sounds. But then you put lines around you and call that a court. You put a net across the middle. Now, all of a sudden, there's definition and meaning. There's a game. There's measurement. You can keep score. A ball is in or it's out. You can assess skill. It's all very orienting. There is direction to the game. There is order and rules. It seems kind of artificial, but that's what makes work meaningful to me. My job is another kind of game, with its own court and rules. I always know where I stand."

Another patient, a man whose need for structure and labels was exaggerated because of an insecure and chaotic early childhood, described his perception of the work world in this way:

"In my job, I know exactly where we all stand and where everything belongs. We have titles, defined roles, certain ways of dressing every day, specific functions and duties, our own offices with names and titles on the doors, and definite salaries. We have clear identities. I am Vice-President, European Property Underwriting. There are 350 people who report ultimately to me, each of whom is at a specific level in a hierarchy. At work, no relationship is close enough, personally, so that lines of authority are blurred. In fact, nothing is blurred or complicated by intimacy or emotion. Getting business and making profit regulates everything. In this company, when I talk to people, I'm Jack Higgins, Vice-President, not Jack Higgins, person. I'm a role, not a person. It's a kind of theater. If you learn your lines well, you're OK.

"Last year, the insurance industry gave a testimonial dinner in my honor. They all made speeches about me. But they're not about me, really. They're about my work. That's the only thing that can be precisely evaluated and applauded in a person. When I come home at night, it's me they're looking at, me they're talking to. Not my work. They're too close to me, and no one, close up, gets standing ovations. Learning your lines is not enough. My presence in the house doesn't mean a tenth as much as it means in the office. When I'm with my son, it just isn't clear who's in charge. Sometimes he tells me what to do! And I have to listen!"

It is not only in corporate or bureaucratic organizations that strict definitions apply and give order and meaning to our experience. Artists are defined, and define themselves, as pop, representational, hard-edge, impressionist, expressionist, conceptual, commercial, etc. They have their own uniforms which distinguish them, and their own language, schools, and techniques. It is their work, not their more personal experience, that gives definitions to their lives.

Another of my patients—a woman, interestingly—referred to the "occupation" of prizefighting as a metaphor for all work. "There has to be a clear sense of your self when you're in the ring. You can't feel, at any time during the fight, a camaraderie, togetherness, or sense of sharing with the other person. You are fighting to weaken his outlines, and he's fighting to weaken yours. And you're fighting to keep your self intact. When I'm working, I've got a hard crust all around me. I know who I am."

The adversary attitude toward the materials of our work demands clear lines of demarcation. In the aggressive position, there are strict boundaries between self and object, no matter how much fondness we may have for the object. It is "me against you," or "me against it." The imposition of boundaries between self and object is inevitable in the work experience; it is, in fact, essential to the successful, creative expression of the aggressive instinct.

PART II

The Love Experience

4

Love, Leisure, and Play

Love is the sensory and emotional experience of *union*. Boundaries are dissolved in love, and we form unities with people, places, and things. The capacity to love grows out of the sexual instinct. Unlike the aggressive drive, which evolves into or catalyzes the development of the intellect, love is experienced through the senses. It is impaired by the imposition of intellect, of words, symbols, and definitions. It is expansive rather than reductive, and is oriented to present, immediate experience, apprehended by the senses of sight, hearing, taste, smell, and touch. *Love is the opposite of work in all respects.*

The sexual drive manifests itself in childhood in such ways as the desire to touch and be touched, to suck, to hug, to hold and be held, to kiss, and to excite and be excited genitally and in other areas of sensory arousal. These sexual needs are all experienced in the body, and come to involve the participation of all the senses. The smell of a lover's skin, the look of a face, or the soothing sound of a voice fulfill aspects of the sexual drive. The objects of this drive, however, are not necessarily confined to other *people*, although the original focus of sexual satisfaction is undoubtedly the mother of our infancy. As we grow and develop, the sexual instinct may be satisfied by visual contact with a beautiful landscape, the sounds of a violin concerto, or the fragrance of a rose.

Where aggression can be seen to underlie goal-directed, future-oriented behavior, the sexual instinct underlies an immersion in the present. Aggression fosters change in objects, while sex promotes incorporation and fusion with objects. If aggression seeks to transform an *object*, sex may be seen as seeking to transform the *subject*. Aggression is a state of being "against," while sex is a state of being "with."

Loving fosters empathy and merging with objects of the present, and an immersion in their sensations without attention to ulterior goals. It encourages rapport, warmth, and spontaneity. Empathy involves the dissolution of boundaries, which is how it is possible for us to feel a friend's pain or joy as our own. Aggression drives us to "do" something (or "make" something) with those feelings, to realize some defined objective. It solidifies boundaries. This distinction is illustrated in the different ways a surgeon and a husband approach the pain of a woman with cancer. The husband who can only try to "do something" about the pain and not feel it as his own, or the surgeon who feels it too much, will fail in their respective roles.

When we distinguish between the two separate feelings that derive from aggressive working and sexual loving, we are making a distinction between two very different forms of excitement. The excitement of sexual loving, whether the object is a friend, a flower, a gleaming new sports car, a spouse, a Persian rug, a Monet painting, or a Beatles song, is the excitement of *pleasure*. In contrast to the pleasure of sexual love is the feeling of *satisfaction* associated with the accomplishment of aggressive work. They are quite different emotional phenomena, and it is no coincidence that their difference is commonly expressed in the old adage "Never mix business with pleasure."

The more sharply we draw such a distinction, of course, the more we can quibble with it. We do mix business with pleasure, often successfully. Yet I think it can be demonstrated that the distinction is indeed sharp—not so much between work and leisure activities as between work and leisure states of being.

Pleasure is an immediate, not deferred, excitation derived from a sense-filled involvement with an object. (The object, as we recall, can be anything other than ourselves.) Mastery, sequence, time, measurement, organization, manipulation, and even verbalization are alien to pleasure. Putting an experience into words is already an aggressive effort designed to contain, categorize, and symbolize the experience, to turn it into a verbal "product." Putting numbers on an experience impairs pleasure. Picasso once said, "If you love a woman, you don't measure her legs." And we cannot truly make love or read a book for enjoyment while focusing on the clock.

Pleasure involves *receptivity*, not *activity*. A patient illustrated this point very well for me in one session, when he was describing a sailing excursion he took with some friends. "When Jack invited me to come out on the boat, I thought it would be great. I thought of all the things you have to do to make a sailboat go. I was excited. But then he said that his boat has a captain and a crew who do all the work for him. That gave me kind of a peculiar feeling. What would we do for three, four hours on a boat? The idea of just looking at the water left me cold. This may sound crazy, but I thought of taking some office work along. It would be a nice, relaxed setting, without distractions. But my wife told me that would be the most contemptible thing anyone could do to a friend. She doesn't understand, though, that the goddam thing made me nervous as hell to think about. I finally resolved it by taking along a load of camera equipment and a fishing rod."

For this man, *satisfaction* could be derived from mastering the sails and the wind, the camera, or the catching of fish. But he could not tolerate the passive, receptive, present-oriented *pleasure* of intimacy with friends, or the quiet contemplation of the sights, the sounds, and the fragrances of a sunny afternoon on the water. The prospect was unbearably dull for him, because he itched for action.

This man lived for a form of aggressive excitement which, in contrast to the immediate, ongoing sensory excitation of pleasure, is a deferred, terminal, ulteriorized, and goal-directed emotional experience. It comes primarily at the end of a linear work process when a task is completed, an adversary is defeated, or an achievement is recognized. Some satisfaction may come during a work process as we see our materials coming under domination and control, and it can be intensely thrilling, as it was for this man. But wasn't he only living half a life?

As I said earlier, leisure has always been conceptualized as the negative, not the opposite, of work; it is rarely thought of as something positive in itself. The philosopher Joseph Pieper, however, is one thinker who saw the essence of true leisure as being synonymous with love. In his book *Leisure: The Basis of Culture*, he wrote: "Leisure is a mental and spiritual attitude . . . not the inevitable result of spare time, a holiday, a weekend, or a vacation. . . . [It] is an attitude of contemplative 'celebration' . . . [which] draws its vitality from affirmation. It is not the same as non-activity, nor is it identical with tranquility; it is not even the same as inward tranquility. Rather, it is like the tranquil silence of *lovers*, which draws its strength from *concord.* . . . Because *wholeness* is what man strives for, the power to achieve leisure is one of the fundamental powers of the human soul. Like the gift for contemplative *absorption* in the things that are . . . *leisure is the power to overstep the boundaries* of the workaday world and reach out to the superhuman, life-giving existential forces that refresh and renew us. . . . " (Italics added.)

That boundaries are at the core of the "workaday world," and that leisure is the power to "overstep" them, is best seen when we compare working and leisuring in terms of the degree of definition required in each. My friend who died on the beach during his vacation was engaging, for perhaps the first time, in an experience which involved no definitions. Feeling the warm sun and the smooth sand, hearing the soft rhythmic lapping of waves on the shore, requires no learning, no set of systematic strategies or procedures, no "meaningful" definitions of terms and operations. It requires an expansion and diffusion of the self rather than a simplification of focus and concentration on goals, and a blending of our senses with the surrounding environment. Eric Berne captured the distinction between experience which relies on the senses and that which is rooted in the intellect, in symbols and definition: "The moment the little boy is concerned with which is a jay and which is a sparrow, he can no longer see the birds or hear them sing." It is something of an overstatement, but one with which I think we can sympathize.

One of the best depictions of "boundary-lessness" occurs in Eugen Herrigel's *Zen in the Art of Archery*. Herrigel, a German philosophy professor, describes his experiences in Japan, to which he'd traveled to learn about Zen Buddhism. His "learning" involves training in the "art of self-forgetfulness," shooting a bow and arrow daily for more than five years under the watchful, often silent, supervision of his Zen master. His objective was to achieve a state of "purposelessness," in which the mental distinctions between self, bow, arrow, and target are obliterated, and only the harmony of all is perceived. There is no sense of satisfaction or mastery. There is only the ability to say "It shoots." The master frowned when Herrigel conceived his task in terms of "I shot it," or "I hit the target."

The Zen ideal is a unity, a melting of all the elements into the experience of a shot. The self "becomes" the shot, and there is no boundary between or around anything. Herrigel describes the feeling of serene but intense pleasure (*not* satisfaction) over the "sharp crack mingled with a deep thrumming, which one never afterwards forgets when one has heard it only a few times: so strange is it, so thrillingly does it grip the heart."

I am not recommending this Zen approach as an antidote to work addiction, or as a means of learning to love, to enjoy life, or to increase one's capacity to enjoy fun and pleasure. Herrigel's is simply a very graphic illustration of the state of boundlessness which is the basis of love, leisure, and pleasure. It is a state which many people who are preoccupied with work can neither tolerate nor appreciate.

I do not want to give the impression here that my concept of leisure is limited to a zombie indulgence of the senses; that it excludes the exercise of the higher faculties. It is more a question of balance and degree than of either-or. Leisuring is primarily about itself, and should not abstract us from our immediate sensations, as is the case in ulterior, goal-directed work. Analytic thinking and focus on the creation of a "product" prevent the involvement, through our senses, in an immediate situation with people or things. The more goal-directed we become, the more we endanger our leisure pleasure.

I also do not mean to minimize the deep gratifications which may come from aggressive or goal-directed leisure and recreation. To be able to enjoy a sport or a hobby, for example, one must be intensely disciplined and goal-directed to develop the necessary skills. But to qualify as true leisure, both the process of the physical involvement and the sensations of the activity must be more important then the achievement of any specific future goal. The activity of taking photographs should outweigh "getting the great shot"; sailing the boat should be more important than winning the race.

When the goal becomes weightier than the process, we are talking about work, not leisure. In true leisure, process precedes product.

For the man I referred to earlier, who was afraid of "doing nothing," even eating a meal was a kind of necessary evil. It took him away from work, and was a form of receptive, passive activity. It was not productive. It wasted time. He could not enjoy the pleasures of taste, nor sense the visual beauty of well-prepared food. Food was simply a means of fortifying him for work. So was sleep, which he grudgingly accepted as a form of payment required to pursue his occupation.

Once we begin to worry about winning and losing, life begins to move in the direction of work. An intense, highly intellectual conversation can be leisuring as long as the excitement of the immediate interaction among the participants is more important than the outcome or product of the exchange. Once we begin to compete and compare, to "measure" the conversation and to "step back" from it rather than throw ourselves into it, we are making it into work.

Minimizing "ulterior motivation" distinguishes leisure and play from work very sharply. This was exemplified in an experiment carried out by two Stanford psychologists, Mark Lepper and David Greene. Their results were contained in a paper interestingly entitled "Turning Play Into Work." Two groups of preschool children were tested for the durability of their intrinsic interest in a certain play activity. One group was told that by engaging in this activity, they would be rewarded at the end with a chance to play with some highly appealing toys. The other group was given no prior knowledge of reward. At the end of the activity, both groups were given the special toys to play with, and two weeks later, unobtrusive measures of the subjects' intrinsic interest in the original play activity were obtained. Those children who had undertaken the activity expecting a reward showed significantly less subsequent interest in the activity than those who had not expected a reward. For the first group of children, the play was partially a goal-directed, ulteriorized activity, and this prevented them from gaining the pleasure from the play activity that the second group enjoyed. Their attention was diverted to future reward, away from an immersion in the immediate situation. Play was turned into work by the imposition of an ulterior focus on a goal. Their activity became purposive rather than spontaneous and immediate.

Leisuring is not linear, but radial or spatial. As psychoanalyst Michael Sacks has pointed out in his illuminating writing on the psychology of athletics, pleasure in sports is not derived from a directional pursuit, but is an experience of fusion and merging. Once a victory is *attained*, we can incorporate it with our senses and derive great pleasure from it. But the primary emotion associated with the achievement of goals is satisfaction. This is the experience of mastery, power, and "winning." It is not leisure.

People may talk about their "leisure time" but, as one student of the dynamics of work and leisure, Sebastian de Grazia, says in his book *Of Time, Work, and Leisure*, "time" and "leisure" are antithetical concepts and do not belong together. Time implies boundary, a compartmentalization of experience into seconds, minutes, hours, and days. It is essential to work, but it can be destructive to leisure.

There are three points to be kept in mind regarding time and leisure:

1. Time is not structured and demarcated in leisure, but flows without artificial boundaries. In fact, there is no "time" in leisure; there is only the "present."
2. Speed and productivity rates have no place in leisure. Products may emerge from leisure activities, but they are of minor importance compared to an immersion of

the senses and emotions in the process and materials of their creations.

3. Time in leisure is, in one way, "wasted" time. In fact, for activities to qualify as true leisuring, they *must* be "wasteful" as opposed to primarily utilitarian.

The "working mind" desires to "make every minute *count*," to have time reflect tangible, measurable progress toward desired results. Speediness involves the achievement of a desired result in a minimum elapsed time. Workers measure how quickly they achieve the result they desire, and the shorter the time, the greater the satisfaction. Attention to this dimension destroys leisuring. Reading a good book or riding waves in the ocean in the fastest time possible is irrelevant to the experience of pleasure. What does it matter if you do your gardening or piano playing *fast*?

Considerations about productivity are necessary and important in a working situation, but foreign and destructive to leisuring. We are not deriving pleasure from gardening if we are concerned with how *many* daffodil bulbs we planted in a fifteen-minute time span. Where quantitative considerations are more important than qualitative ones, we are in the realm of working. In loving and leisuring, it is the *quality* of time spent, the degree of sensory and emotional *fusion* with our materials, which is most crucial.

An intriguing book titled *How to Get Control of Your Time and Your Life*, by Alan Lakein, epitomizes the "working" as opposed to "leisuring" or "loving" attitude to time. As a "time management consultant," Lakein is hired by corporations and individuals to enhance their abilities to "make time" and "make it count." In the introduction to his book, Lakein says: "Time is Life. It is irreversible and irreplaceable. To waste your time is to waste your life, but to master your time is to master your life and make the most of it. . . . For instance, suppose you've got ten minutes before you must go to the dentist. If you're like most people, you'll fritter that time away. But I can show you how to invest those ten minutes so you can make a solid start on any big job you may have been putting off—like redecorating your home or analyzing your production costs."

Lakein takes pains to emphasize that he is not recommending a program to become a "time nut," to become so superorganized that a person is aware of every minute "as it slips by." He encouraged one obsessively overscheduled and overproductive client to deliberately waste a block of time, to show him how "efficient" the controlled wasting of time can be. The client became able to go back to work on Monday mornings feeling refreshed rather than exhausted from strenuous weekend projects and activities. In fact, the suggestion was based not in the realm of "waste," but on a technique for heightened efficiency.

Lakein's system involves the methodical listing of priorities and lifetime goals, and the precise, efficient scheduling of steps toward these goals into each and every day. He puts signs in his office to remind him of his goals, and he reviews his lifetime goals list every day, identifying activities to perform each day to further his objectives. The last item on his "How I save time" list—Item 61—reads, "I'm continually asking myself: 'What is the best use of my time right now?' "

Books like this one have considerable utility for people who are disorganized, only dimly aware of goals, and generally unproductive. But it should not be surprising that these aren't always the people who read such books. The great consumers of "time management" wisdom, the people who want to learn more about "controlling and mastering your time and your life," are, of course, the very people who are already preoccupied with mastery and control, and who really need advice about waste and passivity.

Leisure time, time which is about *itself* and not projected *ahead* to a product or objective, is truly "wasted" time.

Caressing a lover, listening to a Bach cantata, and watching children at play are activities which generate transitory feelings and a sense of pleasure, but no tangible products to show for the time spent in these pleasures. In a sense, loving and leisuring "waste" our higher intellectual faculties. Being able to relax, not to worry, means not to think creatively, ahead of the present, to the "what might happen if . . . ?" Human intelligence involves the anticipation and creation of *consequences*, which are future events. The greater our intelligence, the greater is our ability to abstract our minds to a future state, to achieve goals efficiently, effectively, and creatively. Experience which is bound to stimuli, which is based on indulgence and immersion of the senses in the surrounding environment, is not so uniquely human as working, or goal-directed, behavior.

Waste is the cornerstone of celebration. A two-thousand-dollar bash to celebrate the wedding of two people is an enormous "waste" if you are thinking only in terms of product-oriented, utilitarian ways of spending money. To spend time and money on "celebration" is to promote pleasure, and serves absolutely no ulterior purpose. Some of the most emotionally deprived people I have seen are those whose existences have not been celebrated by such events as birthday parties when they were children. Their parents may have bought them things or taken them places, but parties were considered foolish and wasteful.

To be "wasteful" about someone is to confirm his or her importance to you. This was illustrated brilliantly by a patient who described a gift she purchased to "celebrate" her husband's recovery from surgery: "I went to Tiffany's and picked up a five-thousand-dollar watch. We have a charge at Tiffany's, so I figured I'd just have it wrapped, take it to him in the hospital, and then return it to the store so we could go to the wholesale jewelry district and get the same or another watch at discount after he got home. But he loved it so much when I gave it to him that I didn't say anything about maybe getting the same thing cheaper. I realized that if I had gotten a discounted watch, it wouldn't have meant as much to him as the incredibly high-priced gift."

Vacations are periods of wasted time—and to be truly vacations, the time *must* be wasted. Once we turn vacation time into primarily productive time, it is no longer a vacation. One of my patients once told me that he wished he could go on a vacation without knowing the name of the place where he was, and without a watch or clocks. He wouldn't be tempted to study the history and customs of the area and enhance himself with new information, nor would he be organizing his time productively.

To celebrate beauty in a festival or simply in a loving glance is to eschew considerations of learning and control. "Wasting time" means permitting an experience to be enjoyed without attention to preserving it with some enduring product. Time in leisure is passively lost, with no tangible monument to neutralize its loss. Except for the pleasure of memory, it is irretrievable.

Consider the psychological differences between games like baseball, in which time does not dictate the structure, and games like basketball and football, which depend on a fixed number of minutes for their framework. Devotees of baseball scoff at the criticism that the game is boring because so much time is "wasted." A pitcher can tug at his hat for thirty seconds before letting go of the ball, while the batter may step out of the box half a dozen times, stretching his legs or tapping his cleats, before swinging at a pitch. For a lover of baseball, it is exactly these sorts of subtle, timeless dramas that provide pleasure. The concept of celebration exists in the structure of a baseball game much more than in, say, that of a basketball game, in which it is the clock that dominates the activity, and drives the players to produce before time runs out. When a player hits a home run, his slow course around the bases following the blast from his bat is pure celebration. His circuit serves no purpose other than to commemorate his heroic feat, and has all the earmarks of ancient torch-carrying ceremonies. It is pure "waste."

In his paper "Literature, Sociology, and Our National Game," Professor Allen Guttman has written on the mythic, celebratory dimensions of baseball and its appeal to Americans on some very fundamental emotional level. He muses about the association of baseball with spring and the rebirth of nature, with open, outdoor space, warm, clear weather, and a grassy field. Unprotected from the natural rhythms of the weather, baseball cannot be played in inclement conditions. In a sense, it is a game which does not attempt to master nature, but flows with it.

Time which is structured or demarcated has an expected end point: we know when we begin an activity how long we will be at it. The end is not wrenching; it is anticipated, and part of our attention is fixed on it while we are working. Awareness of the termination of an activity, and working toward it, prevent us from losing ourselves in whatever we are doing in that period of time. This is not leisuring; we don't let go fully. An open-ended leisuring time fosters immersion in the experience. The end point comes upon us with a much more painful impact than if we know when we are going to stop in advance. If we have lost ourselves on a vacation, in a good book or play, in walking through quiet woods in the first snowfall of winter, or in making love, the end of these experiences involves a much deeper sense of loss than when we have contained ourselves by planning on doing something for thirty minutes and no more.

We want our pleasures to continue. We experience a sense of letdown when a gripping novel ends. Our minds do not have one eye on the end point of our pleasures. We have suspended them so that both eyes—our entire beings—are involved in the process and its flow. This is one reason why work-oriented people often do not permit themselves involvement in pleasure. When it ends, the sense of loss must be accepted without the means to avoid it. Control is relinquished. These are intolerable conditions for people whose preoccupation is with mastery and prevention of loss.

Intimacy and novelty are two basic ways that people enjoy themselves, or have "fun," and both have to do with the dissolving or expanding of boundaries. When we say "I love Venice," "I love gardening," or "I love my children," we are speaking of the pleasure we feel in the immersion of our senses in the atmosphere of Venice, the color and fragrance of the flower garden, or the beings of our children. Differentiation between ourselves and what we love fades, just as it does in ideal sexual intimacy—the act of love. There is immersion and union. When friends talk of the closeness and mutual understanding in their relationship, and the profound pleasure they experience with each other, they are talking about a blurring of boundaries between and around them. The concept of empathy is evident here, because empathy involves the ability to "walk a mile in someone else's shoes," to feel what someone else feels, not from an intellectual distance but from *within* the other person. There can be intense pleasure in this experience, in the kind of pure sexual union which is its prototype, or in an empathic, intimate relationship with nature. The pleasure in watching a great play or reading an exciting book draws on the ability to "lose yourself" in the experience.

A brilliant example of "losing yourself" and "having fun" is contained in a description by a professional hockey player whom Studs Terkel interviewed for *Working*, a collection of profiles of American workers. The athlete reports an experience he had when he passed a sheet of ice on a street one day: "Goddamn, if I didn't drive out there and put on my skates. I took off my camel hair coat . . . And I flew. Nobody was

there. I was free as a bird. I was really happy . . . Incredible.
It's beautiful! You're breaking the bounds of gravity . . . I'm
on another level of existence, just being in pure motion. Going
wherever I want to go, whenever I want to go. That's nice,
you know."

Note the contrast between what we may assume his
attitude on the ice is while at work, and here while at play. At
work, his ulterior concentration on the purpose of the game,
winning, creates definition, structure, and an adversary frame
of mind. Satisfaction is the deferred emotional goal. So is his
paycheck. His self is defined and enhanced in his victories. It
is an experience full of boundaries and meanings. But on the
sheet of ice in the street, there are no boundaries, and even
gravity doesn't limit him. It is an intensely "intimate" form of
experience.

Certainly this hockey player could not have derived such
boundless pleasure at play on the street had he not earlier
applied himself with great discipline and concentration to the
development of his skill as a working skater. If he could barely
keep himself standing and his ankles flopped back and forth in
pain, he would never have been so rhapsodic about his
experience on the ice sheet in the street. What defines his
experience as leisure, however, is the fact that once the skill is
"worked at" and developed, he is able to drop his concentration and discipline, and his attention to linear goal attainment.
He is able to "lose himself" on the ice.

"Loving," the experience of intimacy with another person,
is often considered synonymous with "giving" because giving
implies a sacrifice or effacing of self for another person.
Working is not really a giving; it is directed toward the self,
not away from the self. When you work, you define and
sharpen your self-image through your achievements, you do
not blur and diffuse it as in love or play or leisure.

We have observed what intense satisfaction work-oriented
people derive from being able to say "I did it." For work-

oriented joggers, for example, the sport is not an opportunity to feel their bodies in boundless continuity with land and sky, not an experience of intimacy, but a means by which to develop stamina, enhance heart function, and achieve the ability to run a lap around the park in under ten minutes, or to beat a friend. All these are measurable, and all involve specific goals whose accomplishment yields a sense of personal triumph and a strengthening of personal boundaries. But these people are working more than they are leisuring.

The second basic way, after intimacy, in which we melt boundaries, experience pleasure, and "enjoy," is through *novelty*. Two common avenues of enjoyment based on novelty are traveling and joking. No one will deny that changing scenery, or visiting new and exotic places, is an almost universal source of pleasure. By the same token, hearing and telling jokes are obvious ways of having fun.

One of the first "trips" that young infants take is to be tossed gently into the air and caught again. Most babies beam ecstatically at this and would let themselves be jostled and thrown endlessly were it not for the weary arms of the parents. In the abrupt change of position, the infant loses its bearings, its "outlines," if you will, and this is experienced as pleasurable.* Traveling from a home in Chicago to Tahiti on vacation, or just biking through the park, allows us to enjoy a sense of expansion. The expansion of self through acquisition of new experiences, or new learning, is another facet of the pleasure experience through alteration of ego boundaries. Once we've seen Paris, we're not the same people we used to be. We've changed, we've become "enlarged," and for most of us, this enlarging of the limits of the self is a thrilling experience.

*An extremely interesting analysis of this phenomenon in relation to the development of the theory of affect is contained in Edith Jacobson, "On the Child's Laughter," in *Depression: Comparative Studies of Normal, Neurotic, and Psychotic Conditions* (New York: International Universities Press, 1971).

Jokes, in a way, also make us feel as if we are being tossed abruptly in the air. Watching someone who is being told a joke is similar to watching a baby being held and suddenly jerked around. The punch line jolts the listener off his moorings. Incongruities are classical elements in jokes which represent abrupt disruptions of our *expectations*, which are, in themselves, boundaries. When Woody Allen describes a gang of "tough, scary guys walking down the sidewalk dribbling a social worker," we are jolted by the incongruity and the sudden novelty, and we experience a unique pleasure. Our comfortable frames of reference, the expectable boundaries of a description or a situation, are gently shaken, and we are given a pleasant ride. I say "gently shaken" because too great a disruption of boundary can lead to disorientation, alienation, and terror. But there is an optimal amount which is necessary for the experience of pleasure.

Jokes may be useful in goal-directed work to warm up a potential client or boss, or to loosen up a gathering of people awaiting a speech. But joking as an end in itself is alien to the seriousness with which we automatically associate work.

The pleasurable experience of boundlessness in leisuring and loving depends on a prior *establishment* of firm personal boundaries. A vague and diffuse sense of self, a state of permanently weak identity and outline, does not lend itself to the ability to love. As with anything else, you have to have something first in order to lose it. *One must have a defined self in order to truly lose it in leisure or love.* Work, as a prerequisite for the establishment of rich personal boundaries, precedes leisure not just in the practical sense of earning enough money to enjoy your freedom. It precedes it psychologically as well.

5

Mothering

In terms of sex roles in society, there is no doubt that men have traditionally been located at the aggressive, productive, mastery pole. Women have commonly resided on the "loving" end, immersed in enhancing the quality of the space immediately around them and the lives of the people in it. Men have been geared to the long-range future, to career goals, and to the larger world out of the range of the senses; women have found themselves maintaining and enriching the world of the present and the perceptible.

When I observe that men traditionally have earned money to keep the family solvent, while women have addressed themselves to ways of spending it, I am aware of the sexist implications of such a statement. But wives have, in fact, traditionally had the *responsibility* for spending money to maintain the quality of their families' lives. Providing food, clothing, and the warmth of the shelter generally has defined the realm of the wife and mother. The key word here is "maintain." The woman's role traditionally has focused on nourishing and lovingly maintaining an ongoing operation rather than developing farther-reaching ones. It is an essentially selfless role, not conceived for self-enrichment. Personally created "works" do not emerge from this role to symbolize permanently the identity of the woman. The selflessness of the loving role is nowhere more clearly contrasted to the self-enhancement of the working role than in the occupation of mothering.

I want to emphasize that I am not making value judgments here between the relative worthiness of working men, working women, and mothers. Each role has its own difficulties and gratifications. There is no good evidence that I know of that work should be the province of men, and the loving occupations the province of women. In my experience, some husbands are better suited to be the primary parent than their wives, and it is unfortunate that social conventions so often force a mismatched role on such people. We still do not know, however, what the impact on child development would be if there were more fluid role definitions for men and women in parenting. Since reversals of traditional role categories are occurring with greater and greater frequency, the next generation should accumulate more experience to evaluate. Meanwhile, I shall, for the most part, use the term "mothering" instead of the currently fashionable "parenting," since the former conveys the truth of our situation as it applies today, not as we might wish it to be.

In our work-glorifying culture, in which the development of the self may assume quasi-religious dimensions, people have often attempted to identify the mothering role as a noble form of *work*. One patient indignantly retorted to her cynical husband, "I work just as hard as you do. The *only* difference is that I don't get paid for it." But the mothering and homemaking occupation, although it contains many difficult and complex work operations, is not, in its essence, work. To try to dignify it by calling it work does a disservice to its unique properties.

Consider the following case of a woman who sought my help, whom I shall call Virginia Graves. She came to my office complaining of a mounting but confused sense of demoralization about her life, and with the pervasive feeling that "sometimes I feel as if I don't really amount to anything." Virginia was forty-nine and had three teenage children—two sons, eighteen and fifteen, and a thirteen-year-old daughter. An honors graduate of a top "seven sisters" college, with a degree in art history, she had married in her junior year of college. Her husband was working for a graduate degree at a nearby university at the time, and they completed their educations simultaneously. Following graduation, she went to work as an editorial assistant in a New York publishing house, while her husband began what was to become a very successful career in the real-estate business. Virginia and her husband wanted to have a family, and after two years of marriage, she became pregnant. Her income was not essential for the family's support, and in her sixth month of pregnancy, she left her job to prepare for the birth of her first child. It was to be twenty-four years before she returned to a paying job.

For all of those years, Virginia had focused her attention on the needs of her developing children, the maintenance of her home, and the social organization of her personal life with her husband, children, friends, and other family. She took occasional daytime courses at various museums and local universities, had many friends, some quite close, and perceived herself, as did those who knew her, as a happy and fulfilled person.

Caring for and rearing her three children was not easy. Each of them required the enormously taxing and personally depleting attention typical of what young people need as they advance through the difficult phases of childhood and adolescence. But the gratifications were there. Despite the rough spots, each child had a unique and interesting personality, and they were developing nicely, if unevenly, into caring and effective individuals.

Virginia and her husband had had what seemed to be a solid, mutually respectful relationship. To Virginia and to others, the time they spent together seemed to be easy and filled with shared pleasures. One year before she came to see me, however, her husband disclosed to her that he had been having an affair with a married business associate for about two years. He assured her that it was over, and she had reason to believe him. His explanations focused on his own personal tensions at the time, and some successful marital counseling had restored their relationship to a stable, although irrevocably altered, state. In the past six months, however, Virginia had begun to experience self-doubt such as she had never before felt. The first time she had become aware of it was when her eldest son went off to college in the Midwest.

Friends began asking her, "What are you doing now with only two kids at home?" The two younger children were fifteen and thirteen, and her constant availability to them, although very meaningful, was not as obviously essential as it had been when they were younger. Still, when one of them was ill and home from school, she was happy (and so was her child) that she was able to be there to offer aid and emotional support.

Managing the house and the social life, and being the emotional center for the family, was still a serious job in Virginia's mind, but she had begun to feel less and less that she could justify it as "meaningful enough"—particularly after the irreparable psychic strain of her husband's affair.

She heard the question "Do you work?" more and more insistently, and it had a way of lacerating her consciousness. She found she could not answer it without sounding defensive and contentious. The response "I work—I'm a mother and housewife" put most people off and sounded abrasive. But answering "No," or "I'm just a housewife," was just as unsatisfactory to her, for she knew that she worked very hard indeed.

Virginia had the uneasy feeling that she couldn't honestly say that she worked in the sense that "working" is commonly meant. She had liked her functions as mother and wife, felt proud about her contribution to the family life, but could not derive the same quality of concrete satisfaction and accomplishment that, say, her friends who were bankers, secretaries, or architects got from their jobs. Her work felt like a very different kind of thing.

Virginia's occupation left her exposed and vulnerable to rejections such as the one she suffered because of her husband's affair. A friend who worked as a fashion designer once told Virginia that her job, in addition to providing a source of income independent of her husband's, gave her a sense of strength, a cushion against emotional suffering. If her marriage were to fail, at least her identity would not go down with it. In contrast, Virginia felt that her own sense of self was shaky. It depended to a great extent on her husband's status and behavior in the world. The new wave of feminism had undoubtedly conferred high value to paid employment and career development, and she asked herself if she should be taking advantage of her art-history background and working in a museum, a gallery, or in the art publishing field. She wondered if this change could improve her feeling about herself and enable her to have a separate identity from her husband.

Virginia Graves' occupational field is distinguished from others not only by the absence of direct payment for services. Mothering is a separate and unique category of occupational experience whose essence is in the feeling, expressing, and communicating of love. To be sure, there are many specific individual tasks within the role which undoubtedly come under the definition of work: bathing a child, cooking a meal, cleaning the living room, ordering groceries, planning a party, or tending to an illness. *But the essence of mothering and running a household is not mastery and control.* Too much attention to domination, control, and self-satisfaction is destructive in this personal realm. At work there is no such thing as being overly concerned with mastery; it is essential to the pursuit of excellence. But a home cannot be run like a business, or a scholarly or artistic undertaking.

Mothering and homemaking are roles derived primarily from the sexual instinct, the instinct of "being with," of empathy, selflessness, and the experience of joy and pleasure that reside in the context of loving. The assessment of one's self-worth is difficult for people in this role. The self, or ego, is not the focus of sexually derived experience. Instead, sexual experience involves a *blurring* of self-definition, a giving of the self and merging with other objects; sexual experience— loving—is not the "ego trip" that work is.

The "product" of the mothering or parenting occupation is the child. A cartoon in *The New Yorker** shows a dour, tightly vested, starched-collared man introducing his son to a friend in the somber lounge of a private men's club. The boy is standing tall, military fashion, looking somewhat pale behind his round spectacles, his father's proprietary arm draping his shoulder. The caption reads: "Howard is my firstborn, and my masterpiece." A child cannot be a parent's "masterpiece," though, as a set of balanced books, a painting, or a successful investment banking deal may be. To control the outcome of a creative business deal requires a methodical, systematic, carefully orchestrated linear procedure in which there is, of necessity, concentrated attention on the creator's specific desired end point. But the essence of successful child-rearing is destroyed if the child's development is conceived of simply

*Oct. 9, 1978, p. 162.

as the outcome of a parent's management, control, and creativity. Mastery of the "product" and the materials in its creation applies to creativity and work, but not to loving. The loving parent creates an atmosphere in which a child's autonomous development can thrive. If this is work, it is the only form of work in which the product has a life of its own which must be respected *from the beginning*.

Because the essence of the mothering experience derives from the sexual and not the aggressive instinct, systematic "techniques" of mothering are alien to the experience. As a parent, you're not "making" someone, you're loving someone. If you try to "make" a child into something, you fail if you succeed. If they think in terms of goals at all, good parents conceive only the most general and flexible goals for the parenting process: "I want her to grow up confident in herself, capable of dealing with the world, and able to derive pleasure from life." Standards of "excellence" have no place in parenting; if they do exist, their exercise severely limits the parent-child relationship, and poses what can be deeply troubling problems for the child's development.

Many parents mistakenly believe that experts—child psychologists and psychiatrists—can define for them the progress their children are making toward becoming "persons." They expect the experts to know what sorts of specific measures should be taken to enhance the development of their children and solve their problems. Although such information can provide the most general guidelines, human development is not fixed in definition. We know much better what a "good" or "great" photograph is than what a "good" or "great" child is. Standards are precisely enunciated in work projects because clear goals define these standards. If our goals with children are too clear and specific, we destroy the person. When parents are "having trouble" with children, the role of a psychotherapist is more often to remove the barriers which may be preventing a loving attitude toward the child (such as the need to make the child a scapegoat and thus defuse conflict between the parents) than to impart specific advice about child-rearing.

The important, essential qualities of parenting lie not in the area of measurable technique or the application of methodical, intellectual concepts, but in the easy, spontaneous atmosphere of warmth, concern, and love. One's attention to precision and control must be limited, and often repudiated. If you are to be an effective parent, you can tell that you are "doing well" only if you are able to tolerate mistakes and accept distraction and imperfection easily.

There is no "work" in which this nondemanding quality is the ideal, where "experts" have no advantage, or in which "excellence" has no place. It is ominous indeed when parents claim that their children are "model children," obedient, and "perfect in every way." Such parental contentions are tragically characteristic in the backgrounds of young adults who are diagnosed as schizophrenic. The personality defects of schizophrenia are revealed when a child whose character has been formed as a symbiotic extension of a parent's goals and aspirations must make a break from that parent as part of natural development—leaving home to go to college, begin a job, and the like. In schizophrenics, a separate, independent identity has not been formed. There *is* no "self"; there is only the recreation of a parent's misplaced goals. Instead of a person, there is a "product. " A moderate amount of "trouble" with a growing child is normally a sign that the child is trying to achieve a separate identity from his or her parents, and should not be squashed in the process.

We have observed how the geometry of the personal situation cannot be linear, but must be spatial. Atmosphere is more crucial than productivity. In creating a loving, comfortable atmosphere in the home, the mother and housewife must eschew linear excellence. Skill is not a primary attribute. "Mother's cooking" does not refer to gourmet products, to beautifully executed *cordon bleu* dinners. What it most often means is food served in a simple manner that expresses a mother's loving desire to deliver tasty, appealing, lifegiving nourishment to her children. The same concepts apply to housekeeping in general. A homemaker's purpose is not to "produce" an obsessively neat, organized showplace, but to maintain a warm, inviting atmosphere.

In my practice and in clinical teaching, I have seen many "workaholic" mothers and fathers who have turned their parental roles into goal-oriented work. Their children are reared with precisely defined objectives. Toilet training is accomplished with methodical seriousness. The development of skills is attended to with a systematic timetable. These people devote themselves more to *training* their children than to *loving* them. Even though some training is essential, the balances for such individuals are inverted. Some women study psychology to become "better" mothers, and they deal with their homes in the same way. They "work" at cleaning and maintaining their "perfect" environments and marriages. A guest sitting on a couch feels as if he or she were viewing a work of art that should remain untouched. Maids are employed to establish a sign of prosperity, but their work is reviewed or rearranged after they leave. These are very often women who need to discharge and displace great amounts of hostility into aggressive work because they have extremely shaky senses of self. Their work products give them a feeling of tangible achievement that a more easygoing approach to their roles of mother and homemaker would not provide.

But women who appear to be work-addicted at home are not always revealing misplaced needs. The mothering role does not offer easy avenues to self-definition and outlets for normal aggressive needs. The frustrations are enormous, and gratifications are usually deferred, or, at best, transient. Furthermore, greater dignity is conferred on work, on service and duty and obligation, than on love. One woman reported in *The New York Times* how she had put this fact to a test at a party where most of the guests were business associates of her husband's. She was tired of being defensive about her occupation of homemaker, wife, and mother of five. "A Ms. Putdown asked me who I was. I told her I was Jack Hekker's wife. That had a galvanizing effect on her. She took my hand and asked me if that was all I thought of myself—just someone's wife? I wasn't going to let her in on the five children, but when she persisted, I mentioned them but told her that they weren't mine, that they belonged to my dead sister. And then I basked in the glow of her warm approval. It's an absolute truth that whereas you are considered ignorant to stay home and rear *your* children, it is quite heroic to do so for someone else's children. Being a housekeeper is acceptable . . . as long as it's not *your* house you're keeping. And treating a husband with attentive devotion is altogether correct as long as he's not *your* husband."*

The whole experience of this home-centered, loving role, in contrast to a true "working" role, is not accessible to precise symbolization and verbal description. Perhaps that is why only a poet or a novelist can attempt to write about love, while almost anyone can be taught to write business letters or sections of an annual report. The qualities derived from the sexual instinct lead to a giving up of the self, not to a defining and delimiting of the self. They don't lead to the concrete products, symbols of mastery, symbols of the self of the creator, which can be described in precise, objective detail.

A mother is never entitled to say "I did it" regarding her children's successful development the way a racecar driver, a clerk, a surgeon, or a gardener can about their achievements. The exploits of working people can be symbolized, measured, predicted, categorized, and controlled. But a mother has to

*Terry Hekker, "The Satisfactions of Housewifery and Motherhood in an Age of Do Your Own Thing," *New York Times*, Dec. 20, 1977.

stay separate from her products if they are to grow. The old adage "Man may work from sun to sun, but women's work is never done" refers precisely to this "productless" dimension of the mothering role.

A mother's major activities tend to lack meaning in terms of publicly recognizable symbols. Without systematically structured and defined tasks, oriented to precise outcomes and definable products, we in the West have difficulty finding "meaning." When nothing is clearly defined or symbolized, and time flows without punctuation or measurement, it is like hitting a ball back and forth without lines or a net. We can't keep score. The structure of the court gives the game "meaning." A mother's court is very personal and it changes often from situation to situation. For her, "meaning" has to be a very private, self-supplied entity, not easily verbalized, and, often, not easily sensed.

The same is true of all other experience which emerges out of the sexual drive. "Meaning," in this arena, is a highly personal phenomenon which relates to sensation and emotion and cannot be readily symbolized. One of the worst clichés in our information-oriented society is the notion of the "meaningful relationship." For an interpersonal relationship to be a good and loving one, the most important factors are *not* accessible to symbolic definition, verbal simplification, and "meaning." The whole concept of "good communication" is often misunderstood as the ability to be verbal *about the relationship*; "to talk about us." Couples who obsessively "work on" their relationships turn them into symbolic work products, creative mastery-oriented experiences, not loving ones. People talk about "relating" and "communicating," but not about "loving." We have to be content with terms that are imprecise in describing what is essential to a loving relationship between people, or between people and things.

Those people for whom all life becomes a form of "therapy" are some of the most intense work addicts I know. Life itself becomes the material for perpetual work and self-improvement. There is no rest. All attention is on ulterior progress. But perpetual "improving understanding and communication" in a relationship takes the place of "being with" each other in a leisuring and loving sense. And such relationships often epitomize a yearning for aggressive satisfaction rather than an immersion in loving partnership.

One woman described the "meaninglessness" of her maternal role in the following way: "My friend's company decided that to increase business, they had to develop a new corporate identity. They hired some fancy firm for $250,000 to create a new image, from a new logo to new slogans for advertising and promotional campaigns. All of the employees were trained in techniques for projecting a snappy, 1980s corporate face as compared to their old, gray, conservative one. There is nothing comparable in this stuff to what I do. Imagine how ludicrous it would be to try to develop a new image as a mother. 'Hi there! It's the sexy new Mom!' Slogans, symbols, logos, labels—it would be an awful joke."

But such images do have a place in the realm of goal-directed work. A woman artist can see herself as "a 1950s New York School Abstract Expressionist." This symbolic category applies because the painter is creating masterpieces from within herself, delivering products which define her as a person. Even uniforms endow the world of work with rich meaning, meaning which we all use to establish a work identity. The woman who wears tailored, conservative blue and brown suits, simple jewelry, and tortoiseshell glasses and carries a legal-size leather briefcase is immediately distinguished by her "uniform" as an attorney, a business executive, or an impostor. More formalized outfits—of nurses, stewardesses, and policewomen—provide a sense of self through these symbolic configurations of dress which is unavailable to a woman whose "occupation" is in the personal realm.

Codes of dress in different jobs and companies are not necessarily repressive. They often provide aspects of definition which people need to establish order and ease of recognition in their environments. Conflicts and furor do occasionally arise over personal versus organizational definitions in dress. And it is not a minor issue even though the surface focus may be over beards, the length of sideburns, and the presence or absence of neckties.

A woman whose husband had to take over the household and the care of the children for two weeks while she was hospitalized for a surgical procedure tells of her husband's reactions: "He said to me that he felt as if he were in limbo for two weeks. He was doing maintenance work, nothing creative. There was no project that had a start and finish except when he did something like wax the kitchen floor. But even with that, ten minutes after he finished, the kids trooped their dirty sneaks over it and it was just as bad as before. At work, he could have been justifiably outraged if a business deal he'd finished was ruined. But with the floor, he could only grit his teeth and smile to himself, and then go over it again. If they'd been employees, he could have fired them. Another time, the two kids were arguing over who got a bigger portion of cake for dessert. He began yelling at them to stop arguing. The more he yelled, the louder they began to cry. He wanted to keep yelling louder to get them to stop crying, but they just cried uncontrollably. There was no way he could overpower them to control the situation. After five minutes of pure bedlam, he called me at the hospital, and I told him to just be quiet for five minutes and give each kid a kiss. That's what they needed. It worked."

Aggression could not control the situation. Empathy did.

Empathy is the cornerstone and the critical element in being an effective parent. It is an attitude which is by definition "self-less" because it involves essentially "becoming" another person in order to understand what he or she feels and needs. A mother, of course, isn't always in this frame of mind. She must at times be authoritative, instructive, or aggressively task-oriented. But the critical and essential dimension is the capacity to empathize with her children.

Maintenance of a warm, loving, supportive environment does not provide a sense of accomplishment and achievement, except through the triumphs of those supported by it. Mothering is an *enabling* role, not an aggressively creative or productive one. If payment for services were made, the uniqueness of the whole experience would be irretrievably altered. The idea of mothering would be transformed into a product-oriented situation in which ulterior attention would be focused on achievement, defined productivity, speed, and efficiency rather than on selfless immersion in the growth and development of others. When a mother says she feels she doesn't "amount" to anything, she is making a good point. "Measuring up" and "amounting" to something are concepts which refer to concrete standards of measurement, to the world of inches, pounds, and dollars. They more readily apply to our products, our works, our achievements—defined, bounded entities which can be weighed and measured—than to acts of love. A mother is doing something that cannot truly be "amounted" and "measured" on a regular basis because it does not involve the aggressive creation of symbolic products. It is selfless and depleting, and requires enormous strength of character and a very high tolerance for frustration.

Mothers who try to dignify their roles by claiming equality with working women are cheating themselves. Those women who devote full time to mothering should acknowledge and appreciate the unique properties of their loving occupation as being fundamentally different from aggressive, goal-oriented work.

Two ambitious and courageous friends of mine conducted a role-reversal "experiment" in their own family. For one year, the husband, who was a psychiatrist, assumed the role of homemaker and primary parent for their four-year-old son and two year-old daughter. The wife, who had been a practicing architect until her children were born, returned to her old firm. What follows are some of the husband's observations from a diary he kept about his new role and the dynamics of his adjustment. His insights were eye-opening to me; they raised many questions which led to my thinking about the distinctions between work and love, and to my writing this book.

"When I was in practice, each workday had a set beginning and a set end. When you came home, you were off the job, and even occasional phone calls from troubled patients could be handled easily in a few minutes. If I wanted to cancel a day's appointments, if I was ill or had to do something else, I could do that without much difficulty. But in taking care of children, there is no beginning and no end in each day. Your continuous awareness of the kids' needs and feelings defines the role, not a series of specific tasks. There is no way of being truly free of this subtle involvement with them, even when you're not with them. It's a job you can't quit like other jobs. Or ask for a transfer, a new boss, or new department.

"There's nothing that I ever feel I can truly start and finish in this role. There's no outlet for a feeling of a job well done. When I was practicing, I didn't have one job; it was actually many, many jobs. Each patient represented a specific challenge in an overall sense, and when a course of treatment ended successfully, that provided one avenue to satisfaction. Then there were individual sessions with patients which could give me a daily sense of a completed, successful "job," a sense of control over a particularly difficult clinical or theoretical problem. There were just so many discretely defined challenges surrounding me, and each provided a clear path to accomplishment and completion. With the kids, it's an ongoing emotional relationship without any of the demarcations into discrete challenges. Sure, there are meals to prepare, beds to make, galoshes to put on, babysitting to arrange, shopping to organize and do, temperatures to take, and decisions with apparently profound psychological implications to make. But these tasks are not the essence of the job. The job is in your heart, your feelings, your concern with their welfare, your love of them, and that's a diffuse sort of thing."

This man found that he made decisions differently in this parenting role than he did in his former working situation. His decisions were far more intuitive and motivated by mood than by logic and system.

"I asked myself, 'Should I go to the playground or a museum with Sandy today?' 'Which outfit should Gabby wear to the party?' There's no set of rules or system of logic to guide you. It was very disorienting at first. When you're practicing psychiatry, the decision to hospitalize a patient is the outgrowth of a logical, stepwise analysis. You have to be aware of the long-range consequences of your alternatives, which are fairly clearly defined. You are trained for these decisions. You go to school to learn about making them, and the information you gain there is generalizable. The scope of my decisions now is more personal and emotional. It's like playing by ear instead of reading the printed music. 'Experts' can tell you only so much that pertains to your child. The rest only a parent can judge by intuition."

The primary parent role is different from working in terms of efficiency and waste. One cannot submit decisions about, say, whether or not to buy a child a new toy to cost-benefit analysis, as one would at work.

"I remember that Gabby desperately wanted a certain toy that I knew would be in a shambles after the first try with it. I could tell that it was cheaply made and that even if it lasted she wouldn't care for it for too long. It was fairly expensive, also. But I felt that the toy had to be bought because she wanted it so badly and my getting it for her would be very important to her. My predictions all were true about the toy, but those economic considerations were really irrelevant. It meant so much to her to get it. You have to sit around and tolerate all sorts of waste in dealing with the kids: waste of time, waste of food, waste of money. But to try too hard to undo the waste, I think, is missing the whole point of being a good parent."

One of the most dramatically different features of his new role compared to the old one was the sense of the small world he was in.

"When you're working, you have the feeling that your accomplishments have a wide-ranging impact—lots of people are affected by what you do as a psychiatrist and clinical teacher. Patients, families, and generations of emerging psychiatrists are profoundly influenced by contact with you. Articles I publish reach all over the world. It's so meaningful in the sense of seeing my impact on so many other people. I think that's the case with any sort of work. Now, though, my world is constricted. It's me, my two kids, and my wife. There's no visible impact on anyone else, and no direct recognition for discrete accomplishments. This role is a very exclusive thing. It's very difficult to hold up without the outside reinforcement that the working environment gives you, though. I have to really believe in what I'm doing to sustain myself. Loving the kids, loving their growth, their happiness, feeling pleasure in that. There are no award dinners, expanding income, status uniforms, and international correspondence. I don't get specific signs of appreciation from the kids as I would from patients. They expect what I do for them as a birthright, and they're correct. But without the reinforcement that I got at work, I can see how mothers sometimes begin to feel resentful and even worthless. The sacrifice is enormous. In many ways, it's much, much harder to do this kind of thing than to go to work."

He found no significant outlet for personal pride on any regular basis, and had a fantasy that when his children were grown and happy, he would be able to glow with self-satisfaction.

"Maybe I will, maybe I won't. But it's a long time to wait. And even then, it's not like a static product I created that I can look at and take pride in. People are always changing. There's great flux and problems. If I were an architect, I could look pridefully at a building I created, and fifty years later, it'd still be standing there. These kids aren't ever simply going to be a monument to me. They will be their own people. I will have to return to work to create monuments.

"I've got a lot more insight into female psychology than I ever had before. Women who don't work, who 'look after' children and home exclusively, don't have outlets for aggression. They can't say 'I did it' or 'I made it' and point to a specific enduring product which is lasting and doesn't change from day to day. Something that they toiled over and beat into shape with their own wits and hands. I think that's why they sometimes appear excessively demanding to their husbands, or want to buy a lot of things. They need to have outlets for a sense of control and domination. That's what creativity is all about, and everyone needs that. They try to control their husbands' comings and goings. I think that's why Freud asked in desperation, 'What do women want?' They need aggressive outlets like everyone else, but their home-based roles don't give them access to these outlets. I find myself wanting to control my wife more now, know where she is at all times, not let her travel. Also, I'm much more concerned with buying things, clothes, things for the house. If I can't say 'I did it' or 'I made it,' at least I can say 'I have it.' This gives me a sense of possession, of control, of power. My working wife doesn't get excited by purchases. She has her creative outlets for aggression and satisfaction."

The most difficult thing this man had to cope with in this role had to do with time passing and a sense of loss. Every day ran into the next, and demarcations were unclear. There were no ways to stop time in the sense of making something that lasts and doesn't disappear.

"I bake a cake, it gets eaten. I plan a party, it's over in four hours. The only way I get around this is to tell myself that I'm going to write a book about my role as a full-time father. Then I'll have a thing I made, 250 pages between a colorful binding with my name on it. From day to day it won't change, talk back to me, or get older. I think that the reason some parents are always talking about when their adult children were young is so that they can enjoy a sense of permanence and fixity. Their memories are their products. Snapshots. My parents always wanted pictures of me. Sometimes I felt that the photo album was more important than I was. Now I can understand that. They needed something that didn't keep getting older and changing. It makes you feel a sense of continual loss to be involved in an empathic process. There's no control over experience, it just flows on and on."

Someone once said, "One of the minor tragedies of life is that women love men and men love work." My friend maintained that he had never appreciated the meaning of this until his "experiment." *He* was now "the woman." And his wife was so occupied with her work that she seemed to need less of his physical presence than before.

"I find that I need affection and attention from my wife more than I ever did before when I was working. I don't think that I love her more, it's just that I *need* her love more than ever before. At work, I had a clear sense of myself through a feeling of competence, and recognition from my achievements. Now, my competence is an ineffable thing; it's a matter primarily of heart. I need to feel that Ellen wants to come over and kiss me, gets excited by my presence in bed, wants to go places with me. When I was working, all this was nice, but it was an extra. Now it's essential. When she's busy and preoccupied with her architecture, I keep thinking of going back to work. When she's attentive to me emotionally, I don't seem to think about work."

PART III

Why We Work

6

The Sense of Self

It is a monumental psychological achievement when the growing child learns to say "I." The infantile mind does not differentiate perceptions into defined, bounded objects. Everything is one oceanic continuum. With gradual development, we begin to conceptualize boundaries between things, and the most significant of these boundaries is the one between "me" and "not-me," or "self" and "object."

The first stirrings of a self-concept derive from the body. In infancy, we begin to sense our own bodies as being separate from other things we feel and see. Our mothers may leave the room and return, but what we later will call our legs and arms do not. We perceive a sense of self as we begin to experience stimuli from within our own bodies that we can turn on and off with other parts of our own bodies. We may touch our genitals with these "hands," which, unlike other things, never seem to disappear unless *we* want them to, and we experience a pleasant physical sensation that we can stop or start again at our own will. The "mother" that appears and disappears is not necessary for this pleasurable sensation to occur. In fact, it is the appearance and disappearance of all *other* objects in our infantile environments that, by exclusion, confer a sense of constancy and definition to our own bodies.

The discovery and affirmation of self through the body continues throughout our lives. One of the most important ways that we enrich and maintain our self-concepts is through physical sensation. In athletic activities, even the aches that we feel in our chests, our calves, and our ankles, and the chilling perspiration on our skin, contribute to a secure feeling of "self."

Certain conditions which we label as pathological represent an inability to grow beyond "body" language as a means of self-definition. Consider the case of a young girl who was hospitalized because of compulsive wrist-cutting. Even under close surveillance in the hospital, she was masterful at finding means to cut her wrists and draw blood. Over and above the rebellious gratification she derived from outsmarting authority, she talked about how seeing her own blood made her feel "real." She needed concrete verification, from the depths of her own physical being, of an intact self. Because of major disturbances in her emotional development, she could not rely on more abstract sources of self-definition. She was fixated pathologically at the earliest level of self-knowledge—that stage when our only information about our selves comes from our own bodies. People who deliberately inflict pain on themselves are also often attempting to salvage a sense of self from direct body sources. A more common expression of self-definition through attention to physical sensation is the condition of hypochondria. Persistent complaints about aches and pains are often the hypochondriac's only way to feel a sense of self.

The concept of self normally begins to expand during early childhood, and becomes enriched beyond simple internal physical perceptions. A sudden smile on the parent's face when the child appears in the room, a hug, or a kiss gives the child positive symbolic verification of his existence as an actual entity. Ignoring the child's presence is devastating to the development of a secure sense of self, just as a bewilderingly inconsistent set of reaction patterns by the parents can be destructive to the self-concept.

Other parental reactions to the child's behavior contribute to a feeling of self. Setting limits, like pulling a hand away as it tears leaves off a houseplant, have the effect of reinforcing the child's primitive sense of identity. "If I can elicit these reactions in the people and objects around me, I am something." It goes without saying that reinforcement of a sense of self continues throughout our lives from reactions which we perceive in others to our presence and our behavior. Frowns "mean" one thing, smiles another. A pat on the back, a brusque tone of voice, a strong handshake, piercing eye contact, and a punch in the jaw are some of the symbolic behaviors we perceive as reactions to our "selves," reactions which contribute positively or negatively to the way we "define" ourselves. As we develop a facility for language, as we speak and are spoken to by others around us, we begin to collect an infinite array of verbal reactions to our selves. We are described and verbally evaluated.

People who are inordinately shy and withdrawn have built up fears of the reactions that they have seen themselves elicit in people, particularly of the early parental responses. A form of phobia of personal interaction may develop. This is how a painfully shy patient described some of her childhood memories: "My father was a presence in my home in name only. He was an accountant in private practice, and worked in his office until at least ten o'clock every night. Saturdays he worked until five, and Sundays he spent preparing papers all day for his work on Monday. We almost never ate with him. When I was a child, if I ever went over to him to touch or kiss him, he would flinch with a kind of weird look and pull back as if I had some sort of disease. It made me feel weird about myself. He never came to any graduation of mine, even when I was the valedictorian of my high school class. My mother was depressed and angry all during my childhood. She was always sleeping when I got home from school, and if I or my brothers were mischievous in any way, she would threaten to leave home. She said she couldn't take it being with us. It was as if anything we did that she didn't like would cause this tremendous overreaction in her. If we were behaving, she would just ignore us." This patient's shyness and withdrawal functioned not only as a defense against rejection, but also as a way of containing the enormous anger she still unconsciously harbored toward her parents.

The most disturbed self-concepts are present in people who are diagnosed as schizophrenic. Usually, the early parental responses to them as growing children were irrational and inconsistent. Sometimes such parents respond to the child's behavior with smothering closeness, but at other times, the same behavior elicits icy indifference, or even rage. The engulfing closeness with the parent can be so total—with the mother seldom letting the child out of her sight, always holding him, discouraging independence even to the point of not letting him walk on his own, and sleeping and bathing with him—that the child finds it impossible to develop a sense of separate existence and discrete self. The task is made even more insurmountable if the same mother engages in an alternating response of extreme coldness.

The need for a loving, consistent parent-child atmosphere in which the child experiences a warm, caring, uncritical sense of acceptance from his or her parents is essential to the development of a secure, confident concept of self. The general experience of "insecurity" about ourselves, which may remain with us throughout our lives, is rooted in inadequate or inconsistent loving reinforcement and responsiveness from our parents to our selves in early childhood.

Once we begin school around age five, and encounter a new emphasis on skill development, achievement, and work, our selves are no longer simply our physical beings or general responses to our behavior or presence. What we do, what we make, how we perform, and what we achieve now become synonymous with who we are. We begin to expect and to need love for our skills and our "works" as well as for our selves. But no matter how successful we become in our lives in terms of work achievement, a secure sense of self will elude us if early loving from our parents has been inadequate or inconsistent.

Actually, the earliest expression of "work" in our lives is the phase of toilet training, for it is the first time that our behavior is organized around a specific end product. Our parents become excited by our "results" and the discipline we need to employ to produce them. Pleasure in immediate bodily sensation is deemphasized in favor of "getting to the point," quickly and efficiently. The linearity and ulterior goal-directedness of this activity are undeniable. It is work.

The toilet-training phase is the first time in our lives that we experience the imposition of symbolic definition on our behavior. Our bathroom performances are "evaluated," and simplified by concepts of "good," "bad," and "on time." No longer can we indulge exclusively in sensory pleasure and spontaneous physical discharge. We now begin to concentrate on a form of linear, productive, defined activity.

This "anal" phase can be particularly sensitizing in the area of feeling loss. A child experiences feces as an actual part of the body which is separated off and flushed away. Depending on how sensitive the parents are to this dimension of the child's mind, the experience of loss can be either minimized or traumatically exaggerated. The exciting new symbols "good" and "clean" compensate to a greater or lesser extent for the loss. In the child's mind, the message is: "I have lost my feces but gained something else." This accounts for the satisfaction that some of us may get when we enter a number on a checkbook ledger representing a purchase we made. We have "lost" or "spent" money, but the loss is mitigated (usually unconsciously) by the accounting symbol which replaces or stands for it.

Often, children who are otherwise frustrated and even traumatized can experience a special feeling of compensation and praise for their bowel losses, and this particular dynamic may contribute mightily to the creation of work addiction. The work addict becomes obsessed with his tangible work product, and the symbols surrounding it, as a means of mastering a sense of loss and insecurity which may overwhelm him in other areas of his life. An orderly, clean, measurable, visible bowel production can be a child's only means of breaking through a mother's withdrawal and drawing praise from her. A positive response from a mother for "hard work" and cleanliness can reinforce the merits of "working" and set the stage for a later adult preoccupation with work. Even as adults, some people think a good deal about their feces, plan and schedule for them, and derive considerable pleasure from a "well-worked" bowel movement.

In some societies, emotional reinforcement for "bowel-work" does not exist, and these cultures do not create workers or even work as we know it. In the Aranda tribe of central Australia, studied by psychoanalyst Geza Roheim, adults and children would defecate freely and publicly whenever and wherever the desire arose. The only gesture of attention paid to the infant's or child's (or adult's) bowel movement was to sprinkle some dry sand over it to keep the flies away. There was no praise and no attention to what we perceive as cleanliness. It is to their lack of emotional reinforcement for bowel products that the Aranda attitude toward work and work "products" could also be traced. Roheim described an example of their lack of sensitivity to personal loss: "Wandering about the bush, one often picks up a perfectly good boomerang. The owner has simply thrown it away because he is tired of it. He will then make a new one and the loss of time and labor will not trouble him in the least."

In our own culture, however, our works and their permanent presence are critical to our sense of well-being. For most of us, developing and sustaining a secure self-concept does rest with the creation of self-symbols through "works." With the acquisition of various skills, we learn to master tasks and strive to create concrete symbols of self in our work products and achievements. The feeling of our own "reality" is enhanced by seeing our "selves" defined by our works. Freud wrote: "No other technique for the conduct of life attaches the individual so firmly to reality as laying emphasis on work. . . ."

The problems of the midlife crisis and retirement strike at the heart of the issue of self-definition through work. Especially for people whose achievement is symbolized in titles of advancement in corporate organizations, the midlife crisis represents the tailing off of achievement. Corporate hierarchies are pyramidal. We can move rapidly while still in the base of the pyramid, but as we go higher, the space narrows, and there is room for only a few to keep rising. Most people stop. Income and titles hit a plateau. The sense of self begins to be tenuous without reinforcement from these external symbols. In most people's lives, achievement is a continuous need, because time keeps passing, is lost, and we need more and more signs of accomplishment to master its loss. Our hope is that the product of self remains after the time of its creation is gone.

Retirement represents an even more extreme degree of "identity crisis." Without a continuous linear progression of symbols of achievement, time passes unabated. There is no sense of mastery over time through the creation of "permanent" works which "preserve" the past. Even more devastating for many is the cessation of concrete signs of self-definition. To be told that now they can "relax and enjoy" themselves without the constraints of work can, for some people, be thoroughly unnerving. Not only is the external world now unstructured and without specific goals and ulterior purposes, but the internal world as well becomes a confused and disorienting tangle. Without specific work products to define and reinforce a self-concept, many people experience retirement as a stage in the death of the self. For them, the difference, emotionally, between retirement and actual death may be minimal.

The anticipation of created work can sustain and affirm us even through the most terrifying experiences. In *Man's Search for Meaning*, Dr. Viktor Frankl, a psychiatrist who developed the school of logotherapy, has provided us with a touching example of this: "When I was taken to the concentration camp of Auschwitz, a manuscript of mine ready for publication was confiscated. Certainly my deep concern to write this manuscript anew helped me to survive the rigors of the camp. For instance, when I fell ill with typhus fever I jotted down on little scraps of paper many notes intended to enable me to rewrite the manuscript, should I live to the day of liberation. I am sure that this reconstruction of my lost manuscript in the dark barracks of a Bavarian concentration camp assisted me in overcoming the danger of collapse." Frankl goes on to say, ". . . mental health is based on a certain degree of tension, the tension between what one has already *achieved* and what one still ought to *accomplish*, or the gap between what one *is* and what one should *become*. . . . What man actually needs is not a tensionless state but rather the striving and struggling for some *goal* worthy of him." (Italics added.)

Viktor Frankl's "self" was contained and symbolized in that

manuscript, and the completion of it was synonymous with his own sense of survival. Without the idea of having been able to retrieve and resurrect the manuscript, mere physical survival would still have meant the death of an important part of his "self."

7

The Feeling of Security

All of us need some form of consistent loving response to our presence and our behavior throughout our lives if we are to maintain a sense of emotional security. The psychiatrist experimenting with role reversal whom I described in Chapter 5 spoke of the inverse relationship between the needs to be loved and the needs to work. When he wasn't working, he needed to see that his presence evoked loving reactions from his wife, that she would of her own volition seek him out and kiss and caress him. He needed her to smile and express specific verbal approval of his efforts with the children.

When he was working, he felt he did not need this reinforcement to the same extent, and he observed that when his wife was deeply involved in her work, she needed much less physical affection from him. We can infer from this that *work may function as a disguised source of love and affection, and hence, security.* Some people, in fact, thrive on this aspect of work.

In this chapter, people with "problems" shed light on a normal dynamic in the need to work. When something is running smoothly, we often cannot see how it functions. Things often have to break down or come apart before we are able to examine their mechanisms.

When Richard Chapman's marriage began to come apart, his work became its replacement. Chapman was a successful dentist in an upper-middle-class suburban town. He was, to most people who knew him, an affable, interesting, and generous person. He was very active in community affairs, intelligent, well read, thoughtful, and open-minded about major social issues. From all appearances, he, his wife, and their three children were a happy family.

When he was twenty-nine he had married Anita Connelly, a young woman who had come to work for him three years earlier as a dental hygienist. She was four years younger than he and had grown up in a rather unsophisticated, strait-laced working-class family. They began to date a year after she started working for him. He found her quite attractive, and was moved by her naive, innocent quality. Anita was somewhat inhibited sexually, and Richard respected her desire to postpone sexual intercourse until she was comfortable with the idea. She idolized him.

From the beginning, it was never really a relationship of equals. He was the kindly "older man" who enjoyed the adoration of the younger woman. But they seemed to enjoy each other thoroughly, and this balance continued quite smoothly until Anita Chapman became pregnant two years after they married. She continued to work with Richard until three months before the baby was due. Being pregnant and preparing mentally for her new role as mother had a maturing effect on Anita that seemed, in subtle ways, to cause tension in her husband. Although he still cared for her deeply, he began to pick on her for inconsequential things and fell easily into "bad moods." He found reasons to stay in his office later each day, became suddenly occupied with publications and professional activities, and extended his hours on Saturdays "because we'll need more money for the baby's expenses."

Although it was not evident from outward appearances, the fabric of the Chapmans' relationship began to change as the family expanded. They had three children in six years. As Anita matured as a woman, she was better able to express her own personal needs openly and to be an effective advocate for the needs of her children. Richard was superficially agreeable, accommodating, and affectionate, but on a deeper level, he felt insecure with the less dominant position he was now in. He found it less easy to work on his piano playing and photography as he had been able to do without interruption before, and he attributed this to Anita's caring more about the children than about him. He felt that she "used" him to help her take care of the children. She didn't understand or appreciate his needs, he said.

Although he was only barely conscious that it was happening, work became a kind of refuge for him. He secured the sort of affirmation that he lacked at home from his adoring patients, his young, respectful staff, and his professional colleagues, who elected him to the presidency of the local dental society. Work was an arena where he could be in control. He required a kind of care and feeding that his home life could no longer deliver. There, he was called on to do more giving than receiving, and, although he consciously denied it, this made him uneasy and insecure.

Richard Chapman's assessment of the gradual deterioration in the relationship between him and his wife was that she no longer loved him as she once had in those blissful days when she had worked for him. In order to feel that his wife truly loved him, Richard needed overt signs of her affection and support. He wanted her to be able to read his needs without his having to announce them. Unconsciously, he was always testing her behavior to measure the quality of love she was expressing to him. He was pained at even suggestions of criticism, and when Anita expressed some personal distress about her own activities, he perceived it as an indictment of him, a statement of his inadequacy as a husband. He could not trust that his wife or others loved him. He required constant approval and concrete reinforcement, and when they were not forthcoming, he felt rejected.

Sex was also problematic for the Chapmans. Richard saw Anita as "too needy." She desired lovemaking more frequently than he. Richard admitted that his sexual needs were often more satisfied through masturbation than through intercourse. He enjoyed looking at pictures of large-nippled, buxom women, posing "for him" in various magazines. He especially liked photographs in which a woman was looking directly into the camera, as if at him alone. The eye contact nourished his fantasy that the woman was excited by him, and this served to satisfy his need to feel wanted and secure.

Pornography provided Richard with a degree of control that he did not have in the relationship with his wife. He could have, in fantasy, exactly what he wanted whenever he wanted it; any woman he desired was as available to him as his wishes made her be. He could enjoy the fantasy of being adored when models looked directly at him from a page in a magazine. It is not that he had a need to overpower and dominate women in a sadistic fashion. His dependency needs, and his fears of loss and separation, were the primary motivation for his desires to control, to have his "nipple" available to him at all times, whenever he wished. In fact, he wanted a mother's love more than he wanted a wife's.

A mother's love is a truly self-less love where her children are concerned. Richard Chapman's wife had been uncritically adoring of her husband and had carefully ministered to all his needs in the early phases of their relationship. She was always there when he wanted her. When she matured, and her independent self-definition began to crystallize, she found her situation with Richard quite frustrating. She had grown and developed psychologically to a point where, although she loved him, she no longer *needed* him as she had. And although Richard protested that this was exactly his desire, his unconscious needs for her dependency on him were going unmet in a way that frustrated and even stymied him.

Ideally, a mother's love is spontaneous, biological, and uncritical. A mother makes no choices; she doesn't select a child to love from among many she knows. Her love is continuous, infinitely dependable, and controlled by her child's wishes. It is of course true that the mother-child relationship does evolve, and the total selflessness of the mother toward the infant is modified as her offspring grows. But, in essence, a mother's love remains the same throughout life. For Richard Chapman, secure maternal loving seemed more essential than all other forms of loving experience.

The love of a spouse is not the same as a mother's love. It is not automatic, uncritical, and biological; it can disappear as suddenly and dramatically as it appeared. Its prototype is not adoration, but the mutual, empathic interaction between autonomous equals. Criticism is easily expressed, and selflessness is not the essence of the loving position as it is with maternal love. The maintenance of a spouse's love depends on more or less continuous awareness and attention to his or her needs; unlike a mother's love, it can never be taken for granted, at least not without serious consequences.

Richard Chapman was born when his mother was seventeen years old. His father was a fairly successful salesman ten years her senior, who traveled a great deal and was quite popular with women. Richard's mother was an anxious, unhappy woman who had four more children, all girls, before Richard was seven years old. She spent much of his first year alone with him, as his father was on the road three months out of four. She became pregnant with her second child when Richard was four months old.

Richard's recollections from early childhood were vague except for a general memory that he seemed always to be watching his mother taking care of babies. He was a very hard-working, capable boy who helped her when asked, which was often. Two of his younger sisters were sickly, and he did a great deal of babysitting, housecleaning, and shopping for his mother. He had a strong sense of responsibility quite early on, and didn't play much with friends because he was needed at home.

For the growing boy, Richard's relationship with his father was a painful one. His father not only had virtually nothing to do with his only son, but, in addition, he seemed to resent Richard and humiliated him without mercy. When he was not on the road, he was either out with clients or girlfriends or at the racetrack. "Playing the horses" was his obsession, and he consistently lost money that could have gone to the betterment of the family. He had a substantial income, but his wife and children rarely saw it. Richard's mother was always being besieged by landlords and bill collectors, and she and her five children lived in constant fear of the doorbell's ring. She was a woman who never smiled. There seemed to be no way for him to bring pleasure to her, although he tried in every way he could through being a very good, devoted boy in school and at home.

There was nothing that Richard did that seemed to satisfy his father, either. Good grades were scoffed at even if his father took the time to look at Richard's report card, which happened rarely. If his father ever played ball with him, he only pointed out all the things which Richard did incorrectly; he never complimented his son for what he could do right. He seemed to delight in beating Richard at competitive sports which the boy was too young to play well.

When Richard's father was away on his trips, Richard was the only "man" in the household, and he was given responsibilities for which he felt rewarded. On these occasions, he was able to indulge in the fantasy that he was essential to the maintenance of the family. But when his father was at home, Richard was rudely and abruptly displaced. His mother was at the complete mercy of his father. Often Richard came home from school and found his parents making love in the living room. His father would laugh at Richard's embarrassed reaction to this and would not make even a gesture of concealment of the sex act. At other times, when his father was not traveling, his mother would often be out until late in the evening, and Richard would have to prepare dinner for his sisters and put them to bed.

He found solace in school. Here was an environment which was consistent and routinized, an antidote to the chaos and complete self-reliance that was forced on him at home. Learning, the acquisition of skills and expertise, and a sense of accomplishment, achievement, and praise were enormously satisfying and offered him a means of imposing some order and purpose on his life. Socializing was unpredictable and risky for him. He saw people as "takers," while work fed him with gratifications which were controllable and meaningful. Superficially, he was quite engaging and affable, but he avoided deep friendships.

In his adult years, Richard Chapman was, in his overly strong need for love, reacting to life as if he were still in the nightmare situation of his early childhood. Even though the objective circumstances of his life changed and the people in it were completely different, he felt compelled to perceive and respond to these new circumstances as if they were still the old ones from childhood. For Richard, the feelings of disappointment, abandonment, and rejection from his parents remained fresh and plentiful. His life was designed to compensate for these feelings, and he felt compelled to organize it in such a way that he could give himself a sense of maximum control. In his sexual fantasies, women never left him alone, as his mother had; they were always there when he wanted them. He, not his father, was the primary focus of their visible sexual excitement. They smiled for him alone. His attempts to develop a similar environment with his young wife was doomed to failure, because his wife's development was not subject to the domination of his needs for love and security.

But his work was. Here was an arena where emotional gratification was always within Richard's control. The disciplined acquisition of certain skills enabled him to achieve well-defined results as a dentist. His completed, artistically created "products" were a continual affirmation of himself and his worth. This, of course, was reinforced by the adulation of his patients and the respect of his colleagues. Relationships with these people in his work life was sufficiently formalized, superficial, and intermittent (as all work-involved relationships must be) to enable him to feel loved simply through effective work. He was "fed" by his work in ways which compensated for the feelings of rejection he had experienced seeing his mother feeding his four sisters as he stood by. Being contained and consumed by his work provided him with the soothing sensations of being held and hugged by a loving mother.

When Richard referred to being in his office, hard at work with his patients, he would very often use the phrase "in the harness." He would describe the pleasure he felt when Monday morning came around and he would be "back in the harness again." The phrase is an image of passivity, of being controlled and bound, of being driven by an external master. Richard Chapman was comfortable in this state. Even in situations in which it was he who was taking the initiative to create certain projects or events, he preferred to speak of his activities in terms of compulsion: "I *have* to do this," "I *have* to do that." He would say, for example, that he could not see me at two o'clock on a particular day "because I have to see patients then." When I pointed out that he was free to arrange his schedule in any way that he desired, he reluctantly agreed, but added quickly, "I have to see all those patients because I have to maintain a certain standard of income." If I pointed out to him that he could just as well say "I *want* to maintain a certain level of income" as "I *have* to," he would reply, "Yes, but it doesn't feel that way."

It was clear that he experienced freedom as being left alone. Working, even his creative "extra" forms of working, such as photography and music, was more restrictive and "harness-like" than relaxed, non-goal-oriented leisuring or loving. When we work, we can never be as truly spontaneous or free to take the degree of personal initiative available to us in our private lives. Whatever area of work we come to, there is an already formed structure into which we fit ourselves. Implicit in any work task are the bounds based on the limitations of the materials of the particular type of work. Methods, procedures, conventions, rules, and systematic techniques apply to writing a poem or filling a decayed tooth; they are the harnesses we must all wear when we approach a work task.

For Richard Chapman, there was enormous comfort in the "warm" strictures of work. Relationships with his staff, his patients, and his professional colleagues were defined by specific roles. In the privacy of personal gatherings, he was deprived of the structure and landmarks which govern more superficial interactions: he had to initiate conversation without a prepared format or learned technique. His work provided him with a secure, soothing atmosphere which guided him and satisfied his need to feel loved and cared for. Because we usually associate passivity with ineffective, unsuccessful people, it may seem paradoxical that this extremely active, hard-working, professionally successful man was finding gratification of his needs to be held, nursed, and taken care of by a strong parent through his work. But passivity and ineffectiveness are qualities that appear when people's dependent yearnings are given *direct* expression. Such people cling openly to others. In people like Richard Chapman, these same dependent longings are sublimated and *indirectly* expressed in more highly developed, more productive, and more creative forms, but the underlying needs to stay in close touch with a mother substitute are often very similar.

The need to be harnessed, held, and soothed by one's work explained the profound sadness a novelist whom I treated once described when he finally submitted his manuscript for publication. This "product," with which he had been in intimate daily contact for over five years, was now gone from him. It now had a life of its own, and he could no longer caressingly and lovingly rework a sentence or a paragraph or a chapter if he felt the need. He experienced a deep sense of loss as over the departure of a loving mother. This was a normal grief reaction.

When astronaut "Buzz" Aldrin splashed down and left his space capsule after a successful moon voyage aboard *Apollo 11*, he articulated similar feelings in vivid detail. In a way, the capsule had been like a mother who had attended to his every need. He pulled away from it, aboard a helicopter, and had the following thoughts: "During the ride [in the helicopter], which lasted about two minutes, I had a peculiar feeling of loss. It wasn't until I glanced down that I could understand the feeling. Down in the water was *Columbia*, our spacecraft, small, compact, and a virtual extension of each of us. Now we were leaving. It had done its work and we had no more use for it. We had shed it, discarded our cocoon. It seemed small and helpless, yet minutes before it had represented safety and security."* This is a touching evocation of what it feels like to "leave home." The cessation of our work, and the farewell to our product, which is also a "virtual extension of ourselves," can give us the same sad feeling.

Despite his already grueling schedule, Richard Chapman

*E. Aldrin, *Return to Earth* (New York: Random House, 1973).

could never bring himself to say no to a patient with a toothache who just *had* to see him at eleven P.M., or to a journal editor who needed an original article delivered in one week. If he didn't agree to such requests, he would feel he was being lazy or "goofing off," and fear that people would chastise him for it. If he spent more than twenty minutes for lunch, he was afraid that his nurse or one of his assistants would begin to whisper about his laziness and lack of discipline.

The fantasy of criticism always involves a stronger person over us, someone endowed with parental authority and importance. Sustaining the fantasy is a way of maintaining the continuous presence of an involved, powerful, but concerned parent. We are not really on our own, making our own decisions and following our own rhythms, but are still being watched and judged carefully by a fantasized parent. People who say they lack self-confidence and who are overly sensitive to criticism are often people who unconsciously wish to maintain the presence of a critical parent close to them. They endow everyone around them with parental power as a disguised way of keeping a mother or father with them whom they continuously try to please.

The fantasy also contains the wish that all these "critics" actually care enough to criticize and find fault: they care so much that they watch very, very carefully, all of the time. Richard Chapman did not want to believe that he was not the central concern of everyone around him, and that everyone was not watching him with a magnifying glass the way an overzealous mother might. As we saw, his own mother was decidedly "underzealous" where he was concerned, and the lack of fulfillment of his need for maternal caring and concern had a great deal to do with his need to find fulfillment through work.

The sense of being "indispensable" to patients and professional colleagues, which his work sometimes gave Chapman, is another indication of his need to create or to preserve a parent-child situation, not an adult-adult one. Only a parent experiences a child as irreplaceable. The most grievous, disabling loss a human being can suffer is the death of his or her child. No other personal loss, no matter how painful, can rival a parents lifelong agony over a young child's death or disappearance. Spouses are ultimately replaceable. Even more so are workers, or professionals who serve us. No matter how indispensable a person may be told he is, or may feel he is, to his work organization, there is no doubt that he can, in the end, be forgotten. If faced with his absence, Richard Chapman's patients could find someone else to work on their teeth and would not suffer disabling or lifelong grief. The extent to which he needed to feel indispensable to them is the extent to which he needed to keep alive the fantasy of being the adored child of a loving parent.

No viable adult relationship can provide the nourishment for this fantasy. Richard Chapman attempted to secure it by marrying a young, naive woman who, for a time, because of her own dependent needs, adored and cherished him; he attempted it again by fantasizing over pornography. Some men and women repudiate the possibilities of long-term intimate relationships by having perpetual strings of two or three dates with different people. In this way, they can sustain the sense of thrill over a "newborn" relationship, the feeling that someone else is very excited by them. They do not allow these relationships to develop and ripen beyond the early, superficial phases, when their phone call or presence can cause palpable rapture in the other. Clearly, matured relationships do not lend themselves to sustaining this early stage of idyllic fusion.

In the end, the surest way for people like Richard Chapman to be comforted and adored as if by a mother is through the medium of work. The open, easygoing criticism that characterizes home life is out of place at the office, where we are bound by formal, even if unspoken, rules. It takes very little effort in the work environment to become admired by those around us. Richard Chapman was very polite and solicitous to his staff and to all his patients, and for this he was "loved." But he did not have to live with these people, and he saw most of them no more than twice a year.

As we have observed before, there are no awards and testimonials at home that can fulfill the need for, and fantasy of, parental approval. Productivity and achievement simply do not matter very much in the realm of the personal, where the capacity for empathy and understanding and the ability to be patient and giving are the primary variables. "Getting results" which can be measured and applauded is what matters in our work, and what we are like personally is more or less irrelevant.

Outside of the creative or artistic realm, work products are generally not unique personal statements. The "perfect" orthodontic reconstructions that Richard Chapman could accomplish were symbols of himself, to be sure, but symbols with not quite the same depth of personal expression as, for example, his way of life, the kinds of pictures on his wall, his taste in music, or his dinner-table conversation with his family. We are, after all, "what we love" as well as "what we do." Public response to our achievements may lead us to feel appreciated and loved, but is it our personal qualities or our works which are being loved and adored? The person with a strong need to feel loved often fails to make this distinction. In fact, a person can be loved, admired, or respected for his "works" even in spite of his self. Some of our most famous philanthropists made life miserable for those they purported to love and care for.

There was another phrase that Richard used repeatedly: "Let me get to the point." Like "in the harness," this was more than a meaningless verbal habit. Work is a goal-directed or, more precisely, "point-directed" process. "Getting to the point" means taking the shortest and quickest route to the work product or the objective.

The prototype of all goal-directed behavior, the original goal-directed act, is the infant's search for the nipple. The nipple is the first "point" a human being tries to get to. When someone like Richard Chapman repeats his desire "to get to the point," he is not only revealing something about his intense need to gain nourishment and satisfaction from a nipple, but he is also telling us something about one psychological meaning of results, goals, purposes, and work products.*

This is how Chapman talked about money: "You know, one of the joys of working is that the money keeps *flowing* in if you do your work right. It gives me terrific *satisfaction* to see those checks coming in. It's almost like I get *hungry*, then I can *feel full*. If I go through a *dry spell*, where my practice is slow, it's very frustrating. In my personal life, it's all writing checks, paying money *out*. At work, it just flows *in*."

The italicized words here are primarily "oral," and prototypically refer to the nursing experience. Chapman's need to control the inflow of this satisfaction also accounts for his inability to delegate. He wanted to do everything by himself. Where reality dictated that another person had to take over some kinds of work for him—his accountant, his housekeeper, his hygienist—he watched over them like a hawk. Because of the enormous size of his practice he once experimented with hiring a junior associate. The experience was a disaster for everyone. Richard could not bear to let anyone else step between him and his patients. He could not relinquish that control over his source of satisfaction. And his associate was

---

*For an especially enlightening discussion of the relationship between metaphoric language and infantile body experiences, see E. Sharpe, "Psychophysical Problems Revealed in Language: An Examination of Metaphor," *International Journal of Psychoanalysis*, vol. 21 (1940), p.201.

smothered by Richard's continuous surveillance of his work. The arrangement lasted two weeks.

He was also extremely *impatient* about getting his satisfactions. If he started a project, he "had" to finish it with feverish determination. If he read a good book, he would not put it down until he was finished. And he never read long books; short stories were all he could tolerate. He did not have to wait too long with them to feel sated.

Richard Chapman once said, "Working is something I can always hold on to, something tangible. When I try to go on a vacation, I feel like I'm at sea, lost, and kind of alone. I don't have anything to orient myself with, there's no *point* to anything."

For people whose work provides them with feelings of being loved, when achievement stops abruptly around their forties and early fifties, the crisis is often resolved through achievement in the sexual arena. The adoration of young women by middle-aged men, and, increasingly, of younger men by middle-aged women, may gradually come to replace the lost pleasure of public approval derived earlier from work achievement. One of my male patients described the phenomenon as it applied to his own experience: "There was always the exhilarating feeling of personal progress as I kept moving up and up the corporate ladder. I was moving with such speed, too, that sometimes I told friends I could almost feel a cool wind whipping at my face as I climbed higher and higher. I came to this country from Hungary alone, without anyone, when I was seventeen, and I began working as a janitor in my bank. I never had any more formal schooling, so you can imagine what it means to me that now, thirty-three years later, I'm a senior vice-president of one of the biggest banks in the world. When I was twenty-two, I married a girl from the old working-class neighborhood I was living in. I was a teller then. We had four nice kids. Looking back, I can see that from the time I was about twenty-six and getting into management in the bank, my wife and I didn't have much in common anymore. I grew. She didn't. She stood still in her own development, only taking care of the house and the kids. Don't get me wrong. She did a great job. But her work helped other people grow, including me—not herself. I guess the only way I thought I could avoid the gap that was enlarging between us was by plunging into my work. I began staying out very late, either at the office or entertaining clients. The higher I got, the more business receptions I attended, and sometimes I didn't have dinner with the family for two weeks at a time. I was constantly getting tremendous support from my superiors, and my advancement was really meteoric. In what little free time I had, I studied and read like mad, and it all paid off. There were no other women at all during those years, even though my wife and I would sometimes go six months without any sex. It didn't seem to matter to me. My life was my work.

"Along about five years ago, I reached as high in this bank as I'm going to get. I was forty-five. My educational limitations caught up with me, and it was too late to make up the absence of credentials. I've been in the same job now for five years. There's no movement, no wind in my face. There's no sense of accomplishment anymore, and it's as if nobody cares about me anymore. My wife and kids are like strangers. I've achieved a helluva lot. But I need more than that now, and it seems that I can only get what I need from the young girls I have affairs with, secretaries and bank management trainees. I know that none of these relationships is real, though, because once I see a girl long enough for it to become a mutual thing, I end it. I guess I lose the feeling of being cared about and looked up to."

The feeling of security defines our most fundamental emotional need. Its roots reach back into the earliest phases of psychological development, to the warm, nourishing, enveloping love of the mother during infancy. Throughout our lives, the desire for security remains strong, but its sources multiply beyond direct maternal feeding and caring. As we have seen, one of the most common reservoirs of emotional security in adult life is that of work. The mental process of goal-directed, structured work itself may provide a deep sense of protected comfort, as the case of Richard Chapman illustrated. The setting of our work, moreover, frequently reinforces this feeling of security through the affectionate approval of our colleagues, customers, clients, patients, subordinates, etc. People whose early lives were relatively devoid of gratification in this area of basic caring tend to experience exaggerated and unrelenting inner demands for security and love. But their compulsions are only quantitative departures from the normal, fundamental, human need for security.

8

Competence, Power, and Self-Respect

"The joy of work is the joy of feeling our activity *victorious over the resistance of the external world,* the joy of feeling something becoming ours which at first was *obstinately hostile* to our will . . . the *joy of victorious force. . . . The more completely . . . work makes a personality self-sufficing and self-governing, the more this personality tends to find pride in itself alone, in the consciousness of its own force and its own ability.* It is no longer by accomplishing such-and-such a definite piece of work that the spirit finds peace; it is through work in general, any kind of work, *the very act of entering into combat and conquering.*" (Italics added.)

As historian Adriano Tilgher notes in the above quotation, self-esteem is intimately related to the feeling of power and a sense of "victorious force." Competence *means* power. Those people who are deprived of outlets for constructive, self-defining mastery in aggressive work, who cannot express their competences because of racial prejudice and other social and economic factors, often turn their needs for power into the self-destructive aggression of alcoholism or drug addiction. In low-level jobs, where people cannot identify with the goals of their assignments, aggressive power gratification and pride may come more from sabotaging the work or rebelling against authority than from creative "attack" on tasks.

Powerlessness is synonymous with low self-respect. Occupational psychologists are well aware of the need for workers to enjoy a sense of autonomy, responsibility, and control in the area of their work. Those whose work is too carefully watched and supervised are quickly demoralized, no matter what their status or income level.

A good illustration of this is the case of a fifty-five-year-old advertising executive who came to me for therapy because of worsening feelings of low confidence and inferiority. It hadn't always been thus. Ten years before, he had been the president of a small advertising agency which he had founded. An offer to double his income persuaded him to sell his own agency and become the vice-president of a large Madison Avenue firm. But for the first time in many years, he had a boss. He began to lose the sense of control and ultimate responsibility for a completed project that he had been unaware of prizing so highly when he worked on his own.

As a consequence, his work no longer represented and affirmed him as fully as it had before. His boss was a brilliant but tyrannical work addict who did not allow for autonomy in his lower management. All ads, all copy, and all decisions had to be cleared with him before anything could run, and he demanded the right of prior approval about the most routine details. My patient perceived this as an assault against all of his expertise in the field; he was robbed of his creative motivation and self-confidence. To make matters worse, he felt stuck in this job, because at age forty-six he could not pick up and move elsewhere very easily.

When his boss was away on business or on vacation, and this man was relieved of the otherwise constant presence looking over his shoulder, his self-confidence surfaced. He had complete control over his tasks, and the final decisions were his. But only briefly. When his boss returned, his temporary sense of mastery and control vanished and with it again went his self-esteem.

This was not a case of long-standing problems with self-worth, but a situational dilemma resulting in the superficial erosion of confidence and personal esteem. With some people, though, the problem of self-respect is considerably deeper and more generally troubling than it was for this man.

The following case history describes a person who became deeply depressed when he retired early, and his external source of power and pride was removed.

Paul Harrison was a fifty-one-year-old real-estate developer who had started his own business with a small inheritance when he was twenty-three. He became enormously successful, and had sold his company for several million dollars the year before he began to suffer from a severe depression. His premature retirement occurred because, in business terms, it was the right time to sell, not because he wanted to retire and enjoy the benefits of his hard work. In fact, for Paul, the benefit of work was always more work. Each new project inevitably suggested another one. The development possibilities in his work were endless; new goals always appeared to extend and enrich old ones.

"Someone once asked me what I want out of life. The answer came rather easily to me. I have one main desire: to make a mark on the world. I want to be remembered as important, a person who left the world different than he found it. It may sound silly, but a fantasy I sometimes have is to be someone who has a long obituary in *The New York Times*. How many people, what percentage of people who die, get their lives written up there? Very, very small, that's for sure. You have to accomplish a lot, achieve a lot, to get there. You don't get there by taking vacations and playing Frisbee with your kids in the yard."

Paul was a man of many interests. He read extensively on art, literature, and politics, and was a serious gourmet chef. But his occupation was the core of his life, and without it, his other interests had paled.

"I'm someone who needs to be *doing* something to be happy. I have to be active. I need challenges, things to fight against and to have power over. You can't imagine the thrill of buying a property for ten thousand dollars and turning around, eight years later, and selling it for a quarter of a million. The sense of pride and satisfaction is incredible. When I sold my business, I lost this, lost it all. I took a long vacation with my wife, but I realized how despondent I was becoming. I certainly had enough money to live comfortably, to enjoy all sorts of things, and not to have to worry about anything. But, funny as this may sound, it's almost as if I wanted to have something to worry about. Worry gives you a focus and a challenge. You develop strategies, you're vigilant, you're energized and you're excited. I really miss it—more than that, I can't seem to live without it.

"I don't really like this about myself, but I also seem to thrive on trouble. When there's trouble brewing, or problems cropping up, there's something to struggle with, conquer. You feel powerful when you overcome the problem. It's like peace and war. Even though I say that I'm for peace, and I'm devoted to it, I work hard at it in many organizations, I really think I'm unnerved and disoriented by peace. Maybe that's why there *are* wars and hostilities.

"It's funny, but I know that enemies are easier for me to deal with than friends. I don't like that about myself either. I don't have many people I would call friends. I guess friendship is too murky for me; I don't know where I stand in friendship and there's too much I can lose. With an adversary, you know exactly how to operate, what your goals are, just what you want, and you have nothing to lose."

Paul Harrison talked about his life's "desire to make a mark." "Desire," for him, resided almost exclusively in the thirst for sensations related to the aggressive instinct and ulterior achievement. Immersion in the physical immediacy of sexually related experience for its own sake was alien to Paul. But he was an exciting person to be around. His energy seemed boundless, and his interests ranged far and wide, even if he was rarely interested in anything for the sheer pleasure of it. If he played tennis, he had to gear himself for the club championship. If he sat down with a novel, he had to feel, after reading it, that he could write an intelligent review of it. If he visited a museum, he had to read a critical article beforehand about the work of the particular artist showing. If he saw a beautiful landscape, he felt uneasy unless he could produce a photograph of it, or quote a poetic line to capture it. The meals he cooked could be nothing but three-star extravaganzas. He was a fascinating man, but those who knew him well sensed the pressure he felt about "being on top" of everything in his world.

In his retirement, there simply were not enough outlets for Paul's aggressive drives. Those challenges that he could create were of too limited and personal a scope to satisfy his intense longings for mastery and triumph on a grand scale. He tried long-distance running, and became good enough to qualify for the Boston Marathon. But being able to break three hours for the twenty-six-mile race just didn't do as much for him as developing a multimillion-dollar real-estate package in downtown Paris. No matter what he tried, and no matter how he excelled, he had the nagging feeling that it wasn't enough. Like Alexander the Great, he had no new worlds left to conquer, through which to "make his mark." And the agreement he made in selling his business prohibited his return to the real-estate world.

Paul Harrison's early life sheds light on his somewhat exaggerated needs for power, independence, and self-respect, and the dynamics of his family relationships teach us something about how these particular needs are adaptively gratified through work. Although his requirements are more extreme than most people's, his story vividly illustrates the relationship between personal pride and productive work.

Paul was the only child of two extraordinarily oversolicitous but controlling parents. His mother was a "total mother," anticipating his every whimper as an infant, and always available for all his needs as a child and adolescent. She was a woman with almost no social involvement outside the family home, and her attention seemed exclusively focused on her only son. When his parents divorced within a year of Paul's graduation from college and the beginning of his real-estate career, he finally concluded that their only real connection to each other had been through him. They had almost no other interests in common.

When Paul took clarinet lessons, his father not only accompanied him to the teacher's studio, but sat in on the lessons as well. This went on until age fourteen, when Paul abruptly gave up the clarinet, and when he began a lot of rebellious "acting up," as his parents called it. He was expelled from high school twice for smoking in class and being generally disruptive.

Whenever Paul was about to embark on something his mother disagreed with—usually anything which would take him away from her, if only briefly—she would fall ill with one of a great variety of ailments. Both she and his father were highly critical of any friends Paul made on his own, and they always produced urgent reasons for why he should not sleep at friends' houses, go away to summer camp, or spend a vacation with the family of a schoolmate. Their means of dissuading him from such activities was to instill guilt in him about the anxiety and harm he was causing his parents when he acted independently. To top all this off, Paul was unlucky enough to have been born on his mother's birthday; throughout his life, she had referred to him, in the company of others, as her "birthday present," a statement which indicated how completely she felt that he belonged to her.

Paul came to realize in therapy that his need to establish strict boundaries and adversarial distance between himself and the rest of the world was closely related to the suffocating closeness of his parents. To build and maintain a separate identity, he had developed an absolute devotion to work, to the only process through which he felt that *his* concrete achievements, symbols of *his* unique self, could safely emerge. He feared and disavowed any experience which recapitulated for him the early-childhood sense of identity-less fusion with his mother and father. "Losing himself" in pure pleasure raised the specter of "losing himself" forever, of plunging him back to the dangerous "no-self" of childhood. His compulsion for fighting and struggling assured him a kind of independence, and provided a defense against the ever-present threat of takeover by another person.

Because of his need to defy the rigid authority of his commanding officers, Paul's three years in the army as an enlisted man were both stressful and exciting. He felt compelled to commit pranks which embarrassed and humiliated these superiors, and most of the time he was skillful enough to keep from getting caught. He was thrilled with his victories and seemed to thrive on the potential danger of the situations he created.

Actually, the army was only a later chapter in the story of his original efforts to feel free of external domination. He remembered years of being subjected to frequent enemas as a small child to force out the stool which he could defiantly hold onto for days at a time. Outside the jurisdiction of his parents, he often would have "explosive" movements, denying them the satisfaction for which they endlessly pressed him. He continued to play out that scenario later, when he drank beer in a grade-school classroom, or when he had a fistfight with the high-school janitor after littering the hallway with shreds of paper. As he got older, his pervasive need to keep establishing a separate identity was expressed less by self-destructive acting out and more by productive accomplishment and achievement.

But Paul still thrived on danger, on the thrill of "victory" when he took a risk and won. Unlike Richard Chapman, who wanted to keep money "flowing in," Paul liked to spend it in large bursts, and found excitement in feeling that perhaps he had spent "too much." He often preferred disorganization to order and calm, for it defined a challenge. He learned horseback riding and jumping at the age of forty-eight, and competed in riding events in which crippling falls were not uncommon. In his words, "There's nothing in the world like being in complete control of this incredibly strong beast. It's unbelievable." He would repair electrical wiring in his house without disconnecting the fuses, running the risk of shock or even electrocution. But he knew enough about electricity to get away with this, too. And he also had the habit of driving his car with the gasoline gauge dancing around empty.

Paul Harrison had never come to terms with the compulsiveness of his behavior or the true depth of his negative feelings about his parents until he began to suffer from his depression. He had actually been bothered by mild claustrophobic symptoms for many years, but they were never of sufficient severity for him to seek help for them. There were many occasions in which he'd felt a frightening sense of suffocation, and it wasn't unusual for him to need to escape if he found himself cooped up in a taxicab in a traffic jam, in a crowded elevator, or even in a stuffy boardroom. Escaping from such situations gave him a sense of relief and even mastery. Through the analysis of his dreams, fantasies, memories, and associations, he began to make connections between these feelings of suffocation and his early environment with his parents. He had never directly acknowledged his true feelings about his parents' smothering closeness to him and their selfish manipulation of him to satisfy their own needs.

The threats to Paul's identity and sense of self were not only external, in the perceived form of other people's "designs" on him, but internal as well. These internal threats came from Paul's own unconscious wishes (which he disavowed consciously for a long time) to *acquiesce* to these designs, to *become* passive and be taken care of by a powerful person. Even though he could now joke about his mother's often outrageous attempts at controlling him, he was still ambivalent about her. There was great unconscious temptation to give in to her solicitude and the control that inevitably followed it. This was the "internal threat" to the development of his independent personality.

In the course of our development, we derive self-esteem first from feeling loved, and then from feeling respected. Richard Chapman, discussed in the preceding chapter, used work to foster the experience of being cared for and loved, while Paul Harrison desperately needed the respect he obtained from competence, mastery, and control. Where Richard Chapman's problems began in the "oral" phase of development, Paul Harrison's difficulty began in the later "anal," or toilet-training, phase, where feelings of autonomy and self-control should begin to crystallize for a child. It is because of the deep frustrations that each of these men suffered as children during critical developmental phases that their needs for love and respect remained so strong in their adult lives. Their stories do not distort normal experience, though; they merely magnify it.

9

The Conquest of Time

One of the most powerful needs which emerges from early childhood experience (and especially from the "anal" phase referred to at the end of the preceding chapter) is the desire to "conquer" time. We are all faced, to greater or lesser degrees, with the sense of insufficient time. "Making time" for projects we want to accomplish is simply the flip side of the distressing notion that we "never seem to have enough time" for many things we want to do. We also talk about "spending time" and hope for a good return on our expenditures.

In addition to "making" and "spending" time, there is nothing more devastating to many people than the idea of "wasting time." When time passes without yielding something of substance—a completed activity, a created product, a tangible result, or steps toward that result—it may be painfully perceived as "wasted time." An empty "block of time" is often thought of as something to be "killed." If we have fifteen minutes to spare before the start of a meeting, we may have the urge to "use" that time for some purpose. We may get a shoeshine, read the newspaper, pay some bills, make some phone calls, or fill in next week's appointments in our pocket calendars. In the working frame of mind, we always try to have a concrete product to show for time we have "spent." Many people try never to have any "time to spare" in the first place. They rarely allot themselves extra time for a task; on the contrary, their habitual pattern is to try to fit too much into a span of time in order to assure themselves that no time will be "wasted." They arrive for appointments "just in the nick of time." They may allot only the absolute minimum of time for travel from one office to another, so that perfect connections are necessary to deliver them to their destination exactly on the dot.

Time which is bound by fixed schedules is often endowed with greater dignity and seriousness than time which is open-ended. There are, of course, practical reasons to respect airplane schedules and the hours at which board meetings are planned. But many people do not place much value on the kind of unscheduled, open-ended time spent playing with their children or sitting on a beach. "Working" an activity into a schedule will impart to that activity a respectability and a seriousness that it otherwise would not have.

Many people divide time into smaller and smaller "pieces" in order to give them the feeling of having *more* time. Sixteen scheduled thirty-minute segments make them feel more satisfied (because of the possibility of sixteen separate products) than one eight-hour span of time. The art historian Bernard Berenson is quoted as saying, "I would I could stand on a busy corner, hat in hand, and beg people to throw me all their wasted hours." The statement suggests that "wasted hours" were probably much more meaningful and more precious than "wasted days" or even "wasted years" would be. The larger and more diffuse the time segment, the less oriented it is toward productivity.

Time itself may become a product. One patient told me about how, as a child, he would play with his father on

Sundays from three to four, and only then. On the dot of three p.m., his father and he would go to the basement to play with the electric trains. This pattern went on for many years. His father felt that he was doing something very special with his son, something that would not be nearly as special had it been spontaneous and open-ended. We can observe other examples of this attitude about scheduled versus nonscheduled time. Unscheduled time is commonly felt to be easier to interrupt and not so important as scheduled time. A lawyer's time, for example, is considered more precious, because it is scheduled and blocked out on a page in a book, than an artist's or a mother's time, which is freer, in general, from precise scheduling restraints. This point goes beyond the practical factor of having to synchronize more people's time and activities at work than we have to at home or in individual creative pursuits. It is a value judgment about the greater productive worth of scheduled time.

I have been discussing different facets of the experience of time without addressing the problem of what "time" actually is. Is time a tangible phenomenon, something perceived with the senses? Or is it not perceptible at all, but simply a concept, a system of measurement, an artificial set of boundaries designed to master and control an elusive aspect of our experience?

Many of us take for granted that time passing is a sensation we can feel. We often hear each other say that when we are enjoying ourselves, we "feel" time passing quickly. When we are bored, performing acts of drudgery, or "doing time" in jail, our senses seem to perceive time passing with agonizing slowness. When time-perception studies have been made on people under the influence of various drugs, most notably LSD, the subjects have reported all sorts of alterations and interesting distortions of "time sense."

In the final analysis, no one can say that his senses have

perceived time in the way that we might perceive the smell of a rose or the touch of a hand. We may see *clocks*, but we do not see *time*. Many fruitless experiments have tried to substantiate the theory that there is an internal "biological clock" which provides the foundation for our sense of time. Norbert Wiener proposed that it was the brain's electric alpha rhythm, as recorded on an electroencephalogram, that provided the "ticks" of our biological clocks. Others have offered the pulse of cardiac contraction, breathing rate, and brain and cellular metabolism as the internal relatives of the external clock.

Nothing has come of these theories, because there is no such thing as a biological clock which we experience with our senses. As psychologist Robert Ornstein has noted in his extensive studies, time is more concept than percept; or, as Hans Castorp said in Thomas Mann's *The Magic Mountain:* "Time isn't 'actual.' When it seems long to you, then it is long; when it seems short, why, then it is short. But how long or how short it actually is, that nobody knows. . . . Space we perceive with our organs, with our senses of sight and touch. Good. But which is our organ of time? . . . How can we possibly measure anything about which we actually know nothing, not even a single one of its properties . . . our units of measurement are purely arbitrary, sheer convention. . . ."

"Time" is no more "perceived" by our senses than such things as "responsibility," "patriotism," or "beauty" are perceived. All are *concepts*, symbolic constructions which organize and simplify complex experience, labeling what we do in fact perceive with definitions which give our perceptions "meaning." We may go into an attic and pull out a dress or a suit from twenty years ago, something we "perceived" as beautiful at that time but feel is laughable now. We felt that it was beautiful then because of the concepts and standards of beauty and fashion which prevailed at the time. These concepts become part of our unconscious appraisal apparatus and force certain emotional reactions upon us. What is "perceived" by our senses is not "beauty," but a certain hemline, a certain padding in the shoulders, color combinations, texture of material, and so forth. Beauty is an *interpretation* of this perceived data based upon a consensus of definitions current at any particular time. It is the same with concepts like "patriotism" or "responsibility"; we react emotionally to them, but we do not "perceive" them. What we perceive is behavior patterns we have artificially categorized with standards which may change from epoch to epoch and place to place.

If it is true that "time" is a concept applied to, and giving meaning to, some sense perception, what is that perception? What is it that we see, feel, taste, touch, or hear that we organize into the concept "time"?

"Time" is derived from perceptions of loss, perceptions of disappearance, and perceptions of change. When anything changes, the prior state is lost, it disappears. When a sprinter moves from the starting block to the finish line a hundred yards away, we say that "ten seconds of time have elapsed." What our senses "perceive" that is organized into a concept of "time" is the *disappearance* of the runner from the starting position, and his subsequent disappearance from each point along his route. We call that *succession of disappearances* "elapsed time."

Our senses never perceive anything but a "present." We don't see or hear events from the past *in the past*. These have vanished, and our memories of them are merely mental reconstructions *in the present* of something that has disappeared. The "present" is always changing and disappearing. Even when there is no physical movement, our thoughts represent a continuous parade of mental activity. But mental activity, just as physical activity, involves the immediate evaporation of the phenomenon which came before.

Our conscious experience is a unique kind of "parade." When American communities put on their Thanksgiving Day spectaculars, thousands of drummers, marchers, twirlers, piccolo players, horses, singers, giant balloons, clowns, and colorful floats follow each other, one after the other, but all remain intact and survive as they pass before us. Only their prior *positions* change and disappear, as they march along. In the "parade" of our minds, though, one perception or thought follows the prior one but also *replaces* it, makes it disappear from the present.

We symbolize this phenomenon with concepts such as seconds, minutes, hours, days, months, years, and so forth. If you call "time" on your telephone, a voice says, "At the tone, the time will be ten-thirty-six and twenty seconds." *Bing!* "At the tone, the time will be ten-thirty-six and thirty seconds." *Bing!* And so on. Any one of these particular *Bings!* represents a "present" which will never return, which disappears at virtually the same instant that it appears. It's gone forever.

Needless to say, all of this sensation of loss is frustrating and painful. We cannot control the continuous appearance and disappearance of experience any more than we can control the waves in the ocean. What we can do is attempt to harness this phenomenon somehow, to create some sense of mastery over it, by giving it arbitrary boundaries. Loss is the most profoundly disturbing human experience, and it is a constant, pounding factor in every instant of our lives. We continually experience the loss of the prior moment and all that went into it. When people say, "I don't have enough time," or "There aren't enough hours in the day," and when Ben Hecht says, "Time is a circus, always packing up and moving away," they are not really talking about "time." "Time" is already a concept, a symbol, a category aimed at mastery. They are talking about the inexorable passage of experience, the continuous "getting later" of our lives, which we perceive unconsciously with a profound sense of loss.

Our language, and the languages of all other cultures, have their own peculiar ways of symbolizing "time" experience. Our clock is an artificial measuring device which defines an hour as one-twenty-fourth the duration of the earth's complete rotation on its axis. This is merely a convention which has proven very useful to us. One Indian culture uses the time to boil rice as the basic unit of temporal measurement. Once a culture has agreed on a "language" of time, the people of that culture have the ability to organize and coordinate their social behavior, and to anticipate expected phenomena, without an uneasy sense of mystery. When a young child learns the accepted conventions of his or her culture's clock, that child is no longer at the mercy of parents to abruptly announce when a meal must be eaten or when it is necessary to go to sleep. If the child knows that bedtime is at eight o'clock, he or she has a sense of mastery and control that doesn't depend on sudden parental will. Social intercourse on a complex level—international trade, corporate organization, and the like—is possible because of a universally accepted time language. But plans to coordinate the comings and goings of any numbers of people rely on standardized conventions of time.

Time concepts are an inevitable concomitant of goal concepts. Both involve the ability to think beyond immediate sensory experience and to play out anticipated future events. Time provides the future with a latticework to hang these events on. It supplies the "when" for things, and, in doing so, it serves as the practical foundation for goal-oriented thinking. Without time, there is no operational approach to goals.

While time "languages" enable us to organize and master social interactions, they also provide individuals with some sense of control over the continuous, relentless "disappearance" of experience. According to the linguist Benjamin Whorf (who was also an executive of the Hartford Fire Insurance Company), in our language (and in Western languages in general) the passage and dissolution of events is objectified and quantified into units of measure, somewhat like units of physical length, or units of quantity. For example, we say "ten days" in the same way as we say "ten inches" or "ten baskets." Ten baskets can be lined up in a row and objectively counted as we see them, one by one. Ten days, however, cannot be lined up and ticked off in sequence. Days are not objects that can be accumulated like baskets or apples. In fact, as each day turns into the next, the prior one vanishes. Imagine counting baskets this way. Each time we point to the next one, the one before disappears. We are always left with only one, the "present" one.

Our own language, however, reflects little of this subjective sensation of the continuous loss and disappearance of experience, and this is one of the ways that we are able to overcome the grief that a sense of loss would naturally evoke. Our ability to imagine and conceptualize "lengths" of time obliterates an emotional appreciation of what time really is. "Length" implies a static, fixed object that can be divided into units of any convention of measurement. All of these units can be visualized or experienced *simultaneously*. But, as we have seen, this does not apply to time. The unfolding of events cannot be felt or perceived simultaneously. By thinking of loss, passage, and change in terms of concepts of length and categories of static measurement, we have developed one way of conquering time.

We also portray time in our consciousness in a variety of noun forms relating to objective receptacles or geographic regions. We say "in the summer" or "in the past" in the same way that we say "in the bottle" or "in the garage." "Summer" is a tangible "something" into which an event can be placed, just as milk can be put into a bottle. We make time into a kind of geographic location in such phrasings as "at sunset" or "at three o'clock." The sense we get from this language form is the same sense we get from "at the corner" or "at Bobby's house." Time is conceptualized as a region or a location. Whorf showed that the Hopi language retains the subjective sense of unavoidable passage, loss, and change in the events of life. And perhaps as a result of this neglect of time "conquest," they have not developed the technological and creative sophistication of more mastery-oriented civilizations.

In short, our culture transforms the continual "getting later" of our lives into concrete symbols of matter, length, quantity, and location. The Western mind has created a civilization with a strong emphasis on mastery and control— on work, rather than on subjective experience. Our great monuments of art, medicine, science, literature, history, and technology could be produced only by a culture which is dedicated to overcoming loss and disappearance and striving to create permanence. Our attitudes toward death, the ultimate in loss, profoundly distinguish us from other cultures, such as the Hopi. The Western mind is unflinchingly dedicated to fighting against death. Suicide and euthanasia, for example, are not only emotionally unacceptable to us; we have branded them, by law, as crimes. In *The Savage God*, A. Alvarez describes varieties of cultural attitudes toward suicide and death, and these attitudes extend from the "Do Not Go Gentle into That Good Night" defiance of Western people to a serene acceptance of the continuous pattern of loss and "becoming later" which defines life for many other cultures. Still others believe in reincarnation, or a never-ending pattern of cycles through death and rebirth which is typical of all nature.

In our culture, "works" are the most powerful means of mastering loss and death. If we can create a product which endures the passage of time, we are in effect defying, controlling, and mastering time. Our works live on after we die. If we can demonstrate a product, a result, or a satisfied goal representing a "block of time" in our diaries or daily schedules, we feel a sense of satisfaction that time is not "wasted." We have neutralized the simple "getting later" of life by creating a tangible object which does not disappear with the time notation in the diary. It enables us to "recover" the time of its creation.

Some people are more sensitive to the subjective experience of loss than others. They cannot tolerate wasting anything, or discarding the most apparently superfluous item. They must be productive at all times and are anxious about any sign of illness which may hinder their "productivity." The stories of people like these have a lot to tell us about the relationship between work and the "conquest of time."

When Barbara Williams was four years old, her father, her mother, and her twelve-year-old brother (her only sibling) were killed in an automobile accident. She was staying with a babysitter at the time. Until she went away to college at eighteen, she lived with several different families. From ages four to ten, she was cared for by her aunt and uncle in California. (She had lived with her parents in Chicago.) When she was ten, her aunt became terminally ill with leukemia, and the uncle was unable to care adequately for Barbara and his own three children. She was invited to stay with the family of her best friend, which she did until age fifteen, when her uncle remarried and she returned to his home.

Barbara's response to the enormous losses she endured as a child was to become extremely hard-working and achievement-oriented, and extraordinarily productive. After graduating with high honors from a highly respected Eastern women's college, she entered law school. Not only did she become editor of the school's law review, but she also wrote several plays which were produced and published, and did volunteer work for a local Legal Aid Society chapter. She was highly sought after by prominent law firms, and rapidly became a partner of one of the most prestigious firms on Wall Street.

Barbara sought psychotherapy at the age of forty-five on referral from her internist, to whom she had been going for a variety of what turned out to be hypochondriacal complaints. A pain in her chest made her think she was having a heart attack. An almost imperceptible lump on her skin raised fears of cancer. She had been jogging thirty miles a week for several years, and an ache in her knee made her suspect that she was developing rheumatoid arthritis. After absolutely nothing wrong was found physically, her doctor thought that some emotional conflict was behind her fears of physical deterioration, and referred her for evaluation.

Without much prodding, Barbara revealed that she was terrified of "growing old and dying." At forty-five, she had never married, and felt the absence of a husband and children to be painful for the first time in her life. She realized that her contributions to the legal profession would not "last" as long as would a progression of children, grandchildren, great-grandchildren, and so on. In addition, she was bedeviled by a variety of obsessive and compulsive symptoms. She had become neat and orderly to the point that she had to know where all of her possessions were at any time. If she misplaced a pair of inexpensive sunglasses, for example (or if the sunglasses were not in the *exact* place she had reserved for them), she was in a state of anxiety until she recovered them and put them where they "belonged." The idea of going out and spending fifteen dollars (she earned $200,000 a year) on a new pair, and accepting the old pair as "lost," was unthinkable to her. She was extremely meticulous about keeping all of her material possessions "like brand new." She polished and bagged her shoes after every wearing, and had shoe trees for each and every pair. Everything had to be preserved. Nothing could show the effects of time.

Barbara began to keep diaries in which she listed every book she read, every movie and play she saw, and every place she visited. She also kept lists of everything she wanted to remember to do. The pile of diaries and lists defined *her* life uniquely, and also served to "preserve" experiences which had, in fact, passed. *Remembering* was a way of holding onto things.

Despite her large income and accumulated assets, Barbara Williams had great trouble spending money on vacations or other costly *experiences*. It was easier for her to spend money on tangible objects which endured. For her, a vacation on the beach would be "lost" once it was over, while a new desk or a piece of art imparted a sense of permanence. But spending money on *anything* was difficult for her. She thrived on accumulation, on "holding onto" her money, and she experienced a painful sense of loss when she "let go" of it for almost any reason.

For Barbara Williams, waste was the emotional equivalent of loss, and because this revived the grief of her early life tragedy, she fought against it. Early in her professional career, she had considered dating and romantic involvement to be a "waste of time" because nothing "productive" could come of it. She would rather have a law brief or a completed book to show for time "spent" than an evening of fun or intimacy.

An interesting illustration of her feelings about waste came up in one session when she was telling me about a gift she had received, a group of magazine subscriptions. "It was the worst gift anyone could possibly have given me. Imagine having *The New Yorker, Harper's, Esquire*, and *Atlantic Monthly* arrive every month! All those good articles! How could I possibly read them all and then have time to do anything else?"

When I asked her why she couldn't select only a few choice articles to read and skip the others, she was puzzled.

"You mean not *finish* everything? Let good articles go to waste? For me, that's like letting a living thing die. Throw something that is still useful, that has life left in it, in the garbage can? You've got to be kidding!"

Barbara Williams' feelings about "productivity" exemplify that aspect of work motivation related to the "conquest" of time and loss, and to our desires for permanence and immortality. Clearly, tangible, time-defying achievement is a fundamental motivation in our drive to work. Those of us who hear the ticking of the clock loudest are driven, with greater pressure, to work. Our works, we hope, will "beat" time and undo the inevitable loss of self in eventual death. Unlike all other animals, we humans know that death will come sometime. This capacity to foresee our demise, to anticipate dangers to our survival and security, to worry about them, and to work against them is essential to being human. Our civilizations are monuments to our desires to do battle with loss and change, and our yearning for immortality.

10

Amounting to Something

In the course of human psychological development, the child enlarges on its basic needs for security and competence. His or her world becomes a more finely differentiated place as concepts of comparative value and measurement begin to take hold around the age of six or seven. In the so-called "phallic-Oedipal" phase, the child starts asking, "How am I doing?" and needs to get more than a "good" or "bad" response. At this age, analytic thinking becomes finer, and concepts begin to be framed more and more narrowly.

Boys are not satisfied with simply *having* a penis to distinguish themselves from girls. They now have to know how big it is compared to others. Competitiveness with the same-sex parent dominates the unconscious mind of the child along all the dimensions of their experience, and this extends gradually to the world of peers. Ideals are formulated in all areas of behavior and personal attributes (from beauty and strength to intelligence, creativity, compassion, and morality), and children begin to "measure" themselves against more or less standardized values.

The concept of "amounting" to something emerges from this period, and the course of the rest of our lives is colored by our own and our community's evaluation of our "worth." The world of work naturally lends itself to this universal need to assign value status to our experience. It is the most highly defined and symbolized arena of our lives and, because of this, helps orient us to our external and internal evaluation as nothing else can. Of course, status categories are arbitrary and highly variable, but we cannot disown or avoid them without substantially stepping out of the real world.

The work environment is the ideal arena in which to play out competitive strivings. The clarity of hierarchic positions, concrete titles, defined productivity, and levels of compensation gives precision and definition to competitive battles. Most things related to work, any kind of work, are accessible to some form of measurement. A man can feel proud of being rated among the "top ten" life-insurance agents in the country, and there is no equivalent measureable outlet for his competitive needs in his loving or leisuring life. By selling more insurance policies, in simple dollars and cents, he has concrete verification of his worth against that of all other agents in the country. Novelists have reviews, literary prizes, and publishers' advances with which to evaluate themselves and each other. And so on for all other occupations.

The clock and the calendar provide us with a framework to evaluate productivity. Many people measure their personal value according to how much they produce per unit of time. How many deals *per month* an investment banker makes, or how many dollars *per year* he brings into the firm, determines how *good* he is. Those are his products, and quantity is often more significant than quality. There are many who feel that an artist who produces only one painting of transcendent beauty in his lifetime is of lesser value than one who produces fifty mediocre works. In the same vein, if a woman who has devoted her life to mothering *two* children claims productive satisfaction from this experience, some skeptics have difficulty believing that this assessment of self-worth is justified.

In the personal realm, public attention to competitive categories (where they are accessible to measurement) is considered improper and even ugly. Open, defined competition in areas of income, or sexual attractiveness, for example, is frowned upon. Leisuring pleasures, experiences of loving and empathy, the realm of feelings and sensory participation in experience, do not necessarily yield objective or measurable output. If they do, and we attempt to "score" them (by counting and comparing orgasms or visits to Paris), the love dimension is destroyed, or at least seriously impaired.

We need our work, where measurable categories are clearly and publicly proclaimed, to derive satisfaction for our competitive needs. A stockbroker told me, "I'm like a professional athlete. They print my score in the newspaper every day." In one way or another, in all forms of work, all of us have a daily score.

People "measure" themselves in the areas of public recognition and service. A famous person touches *more* people, and his or her enduring works keep the person's memory alive *longer* than that of an ordinary citizen whose "fame" barely extends beyond his own apartment building. It is the same for someone who derives his feeling of self-worth from helping *many* other people. These are ways of "amounting" to something.

It is saddening to read about magnificent baseball players from the old Negro leagues who toiled in obscurity for so many years while white players who were universally acclaimed enjoyed greater access to a sense of self-worth. Josh Gibson, thought by many to be the greatest baseball player of all time, died at age thirty-five of emotional problems aggravated by alcohol. Without the objective, external symbols of "worth" which white players could "count up," his ability to evaluate himself positively was severely compromised.* We all have a need to visualize these objective measures of worth. An internal sense of value from early loving is rarely enough by itself, nor is a private sense of competence. This is why public welfare can be so devastating to some people. They have nothing external and objective by which to measure their self-worth.

If a person with a job cannot endow it with occupational status, then measurable status may come from an association with the value of the employer. In *White Collar*, C. Wright Mills described how a saleswoman at a small costume-jewelry store can be seen as having "less" value than a saleswoman at Tiffany's. A patient once replied to my question "What does your husband do?" by telling me with some embarrassment, "He's with IBM." Probing for more information, I ascertained that he was a janitor in one of the corporation's branch offices.

Another way that we "amount" ourselves has to do with how "hard" our work is, or the measurement of the difficulty of our jobs. Pins which read "I'm a hard-working New Yorker" adorn more than a few lapels in that city. The greater the difficulty, the greater the sense of competence and satisfaction, the greater the pride we take in ourselves. For most of us, an easy job is not as valuable as a difficult one. An elevator operator who works a push-button car in an apartment building once complained: "It's a rough job. People are always asking me whether so and so is home, or what time did Mr. what's-his-name go out. It's hard to remember what apartment everyone lives in, or what everybody's doing here.

---

*His career is recounted in W. Brashler, *Josh Gibson: A Life in the Negro Leagues* (New York: Harper and Row, 1978).

There's a hundred people who live off this elevator! And I've got to check each delivery kid, make sure they're on the up and up. A lot of people expect a little conversation in the car, but a lot of others resent it if you say even a word. Got to keep on your toes. It's a tough job."

It is a tough job if you do it well—and that applies to all work. The meaning of "difficulty" may be understood by borrowing from the field of physics. "Work" is a measurable concept in physics, and its magnitude has to do with the degree of force applied to an object to move it a certain distance. This corresponds to our notions of "difficulty" in human work, which we may conceptualize as the degree of aggressive energy a person exerts toward a goal over a certain period of time. Aggressive energy, as we have seen, is reflected outwardly in organization, manipulation, and control of materials, and inwardly in the form of concentration and discipline. Obviously, we have no absolutely objective categories for measuring organization, manipulation, control, concentration, and discipline, but subjective standards can suffice. *We ourselves* know how hard we are concentrating and how much force we are expending to overpower the naturally disorganized activity of our minds, and the natural tendencies of materials and people, to achieve a particular work goal. *We ourselves* can feel how much force is required to discipline our minds and bodies to maintain single-minded concentration. One way, then, of assigning increased difficulty to work is to increase the expenditure of aggressive energy through these means.

You will notice here that I make no distinction between mental and physical difficulty. Whether we work primarily with our hands or with our heads, the degree of concentration and discipline we apply to a task is the critical factor in feeling that something is easy or hard.

The other avenue to "hard work," or increasing difficulty sensed in work, is through the "distance" across which our concentration and discipline travel. This is the *time* factor. The goals for a bootblack are more immediate and "shorter" than those for a physicist. People would generally assume that to be a physicist is "harder" because the physicist must work "longer" to reach his goals. The bootblack may work harder, though, because he may *attack* his work with greater concentration and discipline. Lots of short-range goals, tasks which require a minimum of time for completion, may add up to a great deal of time spent in one's work. This is why mothering feels like, and certainly involves, hard work. The goals of a mother's day-to-day tasks, as we have discussed, may be short-range, but they require considerable attention and self-control, and certainly do add up to a lot of work.

I do not mean to imply in any of the foregoing discussion that the famous person, the more productive person, or the harder worker is a more valuable human being in any absolute sense. Each society and each individual establishes certain objective standards as conventions for personal measurement. Our self-esteem often depends on how we see ourselves in terms of these standards.

Of course, judging the value of an achievement is often a highly subjective thing. In spite of the existence of objective standards of personal worth in a culture, it is ultimately the individual who evaluates his or her own achievement. The reasons for satisfaction or dissatisfaction with one's own accomplishments are extraordinarily complex, and critical factors often reside in the unconscious. Some people may undervalue great personal achievements for a variety of unconscious factors. Our accomplishments may awaken guilt. We may repudiate them because of the threat they represent to wishes for infantile caretaking and dependency. Some people have such a strong need to keep striving for future goals that they cannot stop to appreciate the pleasure of current accomplishments, and then rationalize this need by downplaying the achievement itself. The feverish pursuit of a goal and the inevitable anxiety attendant to this pursuit may be a screen for the need to generate continual sexual excitement. Intense anxiety and intense sexual excitation may at some levels be indistinguishable.

One of my patients, an extremely successful physician, worked steadily from sunrise to midnight, day in and day out, and still had the keen sense that he was a slouch and a fraud. He felt that his highly recognized achievements weren't really all that people believed them to be.

"First of all, there are lots of doctors who work even harder than I do. And even though I've gotten all sorts of awards for my work, and still do, I still have this feeling that I'm a fraud. I say to myself, 'If people only knew.' I don't know exactly what they should know, but it's a feeling. It's the sense that if people really looked very closely at my work, they'd see that it isn't really great. I can't say I know what 'really great' means. I just don't get the feeling of great pride from my work that I should. It's as if there's something missing from myself that I can't seem to find."

What was "missing" in this man's case goes back to his early life. Both his mother and father were renowned attorneys whose work demands (and probably personality styles) prevented them from devoting much time or attention to the emotional needs of their children. They traveled extensively, and a parade of governesses wandered through this man's early life. Reinforcement took the form of his parents' verbal approval of his manners, his grooming, and his high grades in school. They were unavailable for, and inattentive to, the intangibles of his character. There was no tenderness for *him*, no spontaneous hugs or kisses, no smiles simply for his existence, no easy give-and-take without regard to time constraints and work schedules. His parents applauded at his college and medical-school graduations, but they conveyed little to their son of any sense of pleasure they felt for him. Only his performance and achievements "counted."

In the course of psychotherapy, the meaning of being a fraud gradually emerged. On the one hand, it related to feeling "incomplete" as a person without a concrete sense of parental love. "It's like I'm not really whole. Strangers and my admirers think that I am. But if I were, I would have memories to call forth of a sense of closeness and acceptance with my parents. My mother never showed real affection for me. And even though my father has praised my accomplishments, I never really believed him. It was as if he said it just in passing. I don't have parents who are part of me." He once compared himself to a willow tree which may be impressive and beautiful to look at, but has very shallow roots and is easily blown over in a strong wind.

Another meaning of "fraud" for this man came from the feeling he had that people saw him as strong and proud. The misrepresentation here is in the fact that, to himself, he was not strong, but weakly dependent on the signs of affection and approval he got from patients and colleagues. He was a man who wanted desperately to be liked, to compensate for the profound sense of absent love in his early life.

The third level of "fraudulence" for this patient was in the concealment of his rage and hostility. The anger at his self-centered parents, which became conscious during the therapy, was actually spread to all the people in his life. He felt a condescending animosity even toward his admirers. In his "if they only knew" fantasy, he expressed, unconsciously, the attitude of bitter scorn toward "the dopes who have been taken in by me."

This man could not feel that he "amounted" to something no matter how effective or successful his work was. He was not endowed with a necessary emotional prerequisite: the basic experience of early parental love and acceptance. Another prerequisite for the ability to believe in the value of one's own successes is the prior sense of competence in the area of recognition. Some people who do not have a basic sense of personal mastery will often attribute their achievements to lucky breaks, connections, etc.

No one can truly build a sturdy edifice above a shaky and insecure foundation. When the foundation of early love and competence is there, however, the feeling of self-esteem is finally *completed* by seeing our selves reflected in measurable achievement. Tangible work accomplishment is the major way that we evaluate ourselves, and no one can escape or deny the need to do this.

Our psychological destinies as human beings are established by our mental endowments. As long as we are gifted with the ability to think symbolically, to use concepts of number and comparative measurement, we are fated to apply these capacities to our life experience. We all give ourselves grades, in one way or another, throughout our lives. Work achievement provides the most easily perceptible symbols for the evaluation of self-worth. It is by no means the only source of personal quantification, but it is undoubtedly the central one.

PART IV

Imbalance

11

The Addiction to Work

The critical factor in defining "work addiction" is the level of choice and free will in a person's work habits. *An addiction is measured not by what an individual does, but by what he or she cannot do.* A wine lover may thrill to the bouquet, texture, and taste of the best Bordeaux night after night with his supper, but he is not an addict unless he cannot *not* drink wine if circumstances call for abstinence, if wine is not easily available, or if his conscious desire is not to drink at a particular time. By the same token, a person who loves his or her work passionately, who experiences the gratifications of achievement with profound satisfaction, and who works hard and long at what he or she identifies as goals is not necessarily a work addict. Only if such a person cannot do *without* the excitement of work when such excitement is not appropriate or consciously desirable can we call him or her an addict.

For some people, as we have seen, work can be just as strong a narcotic as heroin in terms of its mood-altering properties. If we see that a heroin user cannot stop taking the drug when he consciously tries to stop, we diagnose heroin addiction. When a person must work while sleeping or instead of sleeping, while eating, while making love or reading a novel, while talking to friends or playing with his children, while swimming, sipping wine, or taking a walk through the autumn woods, he is revealing what he *cannot* do. The work addict has no choice in the matter, even when he wants to change. *He cannot stop working.*

We need to make a distinction between chronic work addiction and periodic "binge" addiction. Like the chronic alcoholic, the chronic work addict has developed a characteristic personality and life-style based on the indulgence of his addiction. His life is defined by his work pattern. All other activities and relationships are secondary. The pattern is so long-standing that one is unable to assign psychological motives to his current behavior based on circumstances in the present. His need for work is embedded in factors that go back to early childhood and seems independent of the stresses he may be experiencing at any present time. His life is in one groove, and it is hard to identify more than one reaction pattern to the various events he experiences in his life. He reacts the same way to everything. He celebrates his successes and punishes his failures with more and more work.

The "binge," or transient, work addict is in more reactive contact with his current environment. His work intensity ebbs and flows depending on the circumstances of the present and on his emotional susceptibilities. There are many times in a person's life when work may become temporarily addictive —may seem to be the only way of resolving stressful or painful situations.

One man went on a work binge following the birth of his first child. Indignation at the dislocations and rejections he felt at home catapulted him to his office, where he found a reliable source of self-affirmation. He was still "somebody" to his clients and colleagues, while at home he seemed no more than a bystander. Whatever anger he contained at home, he was able to discharge through an aggressive "attack" on problems in his office. He realized that his working was becoming addictive when he sadly found himself preferring to see clients in his office during evenings and on weekends instead of enjoying his wife and newborn child. He was very distressed by this. Gradually, he came to realize that he was reacting not so much to the objective realities of the present situation as to feelings related to having been an only child. He was motivated by jealousies that stemmed from needs to be cared for and nurtured by his wife as if she were his mother. He found in his work what he felt she was denying him. Understanding these determinants helped him to overcome his temporary compulsion and brought him closer to his wife and son.

It is easy enough to say that a work addict reveals his addiction by what he *cannot* do, but how do we know when this is the case? One of the most characteristic traits of all addicts, whether they are hooked on alcohol, heroin, or work, is that they often assiduously deny, or are truly unaware, that they are not in control of their habits. "I can stop anytime I want." It is not that they are lying. Most of them are actually not conscious of their addiction. Those that are conscious of a compulsion for work will come forward directly and describe the subjective pain associated with the cessation of work. They clearly outline the withdrawal symptoms which they can anticipate and need to ward off. These symptoms include intense anxiety (often associated with shortness of breath, tremulousness, perspiration, cold, clammy palms, and loss of appetite), depression (feelings of hopelessness, despair, loss of will to live, intense guilt, sleeplessness, appetite loss, and disappearance of all interests, including sex), psychosomatic illnesses (migraine, colitis, asthma, duodenal ulcer, etc.), or even frank psychoses (loss of ability to distinguish reality from fantasy, as seen in delusions, hallucinations, and incoherent speech).

If the work addict does not supply this subjective information about himself, we must assume the presence of addiction by inference from objective data. These include, of course, the appearance of the above symptoms when work ceases for short or long periods because of illness, unemployment, vacations, weekends, sleep, mealtime, or other circumstances beyond the person's control. Withdrawal may occur during a period of mourning following the death of a family member, or even during the forced inactivity of a traffic jam, when no journals or dictaphone have been brought along to ward off the unanticipated work stoppage.

We may also infer the presence of an addiction from the appearance of medical illness as a direct result of overwork. This, of course, is much easier to ascertain when we are dealing with addiction to toxic substances, such as alcohol, which cause predictable changes in such organs as the liver, the pancreas, and the brain. But, oddly enough, many work addicts are large consumers of such drugs as alcohol and marijuana, because these are the only means by which they can wrench themselves away from their compulsive work orientation. And while there are many addicts who launch themselves into physical-fitness regimens with a determined working attitude (with specific exercise, nutrition, and sleep programs), there are others who neglect their health because of their obsessive concentration on their jobs. They begin to show signs of physical deterioration. They may smoke several packs of cigarettes a day, drink too much alcohol, or become overweight from eating too much starchy, filling food on the run. Lack of sleep may catch up with them physically, and accidents may occur with greater frequency, leading to serious injury.

There is a third way we may infer the presence of an addiction—by noting problems in psychosocial adaptation. Is there a breakdown or impairment in areas of subjective self-worth, relations with family and friends, and in one's work? This is the knottiest criterion, because, of course, it cannot truly be standardized. By whose definition can one say that a person's functioning is impaired? The only reliable definition is that of the addict himself, but his opinion is rarely objective. Certainly, in severe cases in which a person hates himself for his inability to control his compulsive need for work, in which his work pattern has clearly destroyed a marriage and a family, in which children are neglected and become seriously disturbed, and in which achievement in work is impaired because the addict is always so busy that he cannot ever take time to reflect on his goals, it is easy to consider this pathological. But most cases are not so clear-cut.

Who, after all, is to say that optimal functioning must include harmonious family relationships, easygoing friendships, and children of one's own? What about the person who asserts, candidly and without defensiveness, that marriage, children, and friends are of much less importance in the scheme of her life than the successful creation of great art? There is only one truly reliable standard to employ in affixing the label "maladaptive," and that is the subjective one.

Psychiatrists must be guided by where a person *says* it hurts, not by where we think it should hurt. The person who wants to marry but whose uncontrollable concentration on work always stands in the way of the successful development of a relationship, feels his or her work habit to be maladaptive. Such a person is in conflict with his or her *own* standards and desires. This does not mean that one should always take what a person says at face value. Someone may assert that friends aren't important, but a good psychiatrist is able to ascertain whether or not this is a defensive statement. He can elicit from the patient the fact that he or she does, in truth, want to have friends, but that fears of rejection, for example, stand in the way of seeking them out.

Subjective distress with one's own life adaptation may arise only after certain events occur which force a person to examine himself and think about the standards he has unconsciously established to structure his life. One man who had always blamed his wife's "dependency" on him as the cause of his inability to reach the top of the corporate ladder, and who had always secretly wished that he had never married, came to realize, after her sudden death, that, in fact, his life felt empty without the stimulation of her presence. His motivation for work deteriorated drastically. Some people come to question their values, like the primacy of work achievement, only after they begin to associate such tragedies as a child's suicide or severely delinquent behavior with their own compulsive work patterns. Others have come for help after reading the increasingly popular "checklists for work-aholics," which appear from time to time in magazines and newspapers. The value of such checklists is not in their pretense of absolute definition, but in their usefulness as catalysts for self-reflection.

Of course, one of the most powerful factors to inspire self-examination is the passage of time—advancing age, and the midlife "crisis." The "gut-level" acknowledgment, in the late thirties and forties, that we will not live forever, that there is not enough time for all roads to be traveled, and that we must begin to be selective about where we want to devote our energies in our remaining years, leads to a questioning about what kind of people we have been and want to be. Some people come to feel that they have indeed been addicted to work, or have emphasized a working attitude toward life that may be at odds, if it is too pervasive and intense, with a loving attitude. They may come to realize that their concentration on mastery and control has virtually obliterated all other forms of experience, particularly those in which the lessening of control is necessary for gratification. They may be forced into acknowledging that their emphasis on work and achievement is truly obsessive and not subject to the power of their will. They may perceive that their work patterns are an involuntary personality reaction, not to the objective realities of life in the present, but to traumatic experiences from the past, kept alive in their unconscious minds. This is the essence of neurosis, and true work addiction—an inability to stop the continuous working at one's life—certainly qualifies as a neurosis.

We have defined work as *the skillful organization, manipulation, and control of the external and internal environments to achieve a desired goal most efficiently and effectively.* There are clearly many aspects to the process of work, and many phases through which this process passes over time. There is no typical work addict, because each one finds something different about work that gratifies an addictive, neurotic need. Some relish the aggressiveness of work, while others depend on the order it provides, into which they can passively fit. Some are obsessed with the initiation phase of work, but never follow through to the achievement phase. Still others draw sustenance from the narcotizing effects of concentration, but rely on people in authority to define and initiate tasks for them. And there are those with strong competitive needs for whom work means victory, and the satisfaction of being "better" than other people.

Notwithstanding these significant differences from individual to individual over what aspect of work fills a person's addictive need, a general profile of the work addict does emerge, and can be utilized as a simple screening device. As with all other screening devices, it is not a final diagnostic test; it merely alerts us to areas that may deserve more detailed examination.

1. A work addict has an involuntary predilection for skills and skill development, and either applies them where they do not belong or avoids situations in which skill is not a factor. He is uncomfortable with such qualities as emotion, fantasy, and spontaneity because they involve no skill and are instead immediate experiences which require no special goal-defined

talents. (People sometimes are heard to talk about the needs to improve their "emotional skills" or "intimacy skills." This is a misguided application of the concept of therapy, but it does attract many work addicts to therapies which focus on "games" people play, and which cater to their skill orientation.)

2. A work addict's mind is oriented almost exclusively to the analytic attitude, which breaks down experience into manageable categories. He is obsessed with precise definitions, goals, policies, facts, lists, measurements, methods, procedures, and strategies. He either avoids any experience which is not accessible to analytic breakdown, or tries to force it into an analytic mold. He cannot accept "the indescribable." Those who need to *define* love before permitting themselves to love or be loved exhibit this quality of work addiction.

3. A work addict is a creature of the aggressive instinct. "Manipulation and control" of his environment provides him with the feeling of satisfaction and pride. Concentration and discipline represent a form of self-directed aggression which reinforces the sense of satisfaction. A work addict cannot leave anything alone. One of my patients cannot see a movie or read a book without constantly thinking how he would have done it differently. He cannot sit back and enjoy; he "attacks" everything.

4. The work addict cannot live in the present. Goals and products, the end points of the linear work process, define his consciousness. His life is embedded in ulterior motives, moving always toward something, rarely stopping to enjoy the sensations of the present. If it is to have value for him, time must either yield products or contribute to their creation. Experience which is "about itself," such as leisure, is irrelevant to the work addict.

5. Efficiency and effectiveness are part of the religion of the work addict. Waste and loss of any kind are not only to be

avoided, they are profoundly upsetting. Goals must be achieved in the shortest possible time with minimum expenditure of materials. Although efficiency is the stated objective of the work addict, he is often hopelessly inefficient because of his need to expend aggressive energy and because of his perfectionism. If he delegates work to another person or to a machine, he is surrendering highly valued control.

Once we have been able to identify a work addict from this general screening profile, we need a more precise typology to distinguish the particular emotional landscape that characterizes him or her. This is critical to the assessment of prognosis and mode of treatment. The most useful typology for therapeutic purposes is one that is based not on surface behavior, but on the underlying psychodynamics of an individual's motivation to work. Work is a process with many parts and properties, and each facet is available to gratify normal needs or to build an addiction upon. The exaggeratedly intense needs of the work addict only give us graphic, vivid, "blown-up" examples of the normal gratifications of work.

By proposing the following classification of work addicts, I am not sitting in judgment from my position "on high" and identifying a group of "sick" people. All human behavior, including that of psychiatrists, is understandable on the basis of realistic reactions to the current environment, as well as in terms of reactions to various antecedents from the past. As psychiatrist Harry Stack Sullivan once said, "We are all more human than otherwise." All of us are susceptible to neurosis, and all of us may find ourselves, at one time or another in our lives, excessively attached to our work. Those of us who have reacted in this manner are not to be labeled as "sick" or accused and patronized as pathological, nor should we feel ashamed that our behavior may be motivated by forces outside of our conscious awareness. There is no easy distinction between illness and health in the area of human emotions and behavior, and all of us ought to be grateful for that.

The dynamics described in what follows refer to both chronic and temporary forms of work addiction. For want of a better system, I have ordered the categories alphabetically; many of them, of course, overlap. The category of "narcissistic work addict" is discussed separately in Chapter 12.

1. THE ANGRY, HOSTILE WORK ADDICT

Work functions as an adaptive, socially acceptable means of discharging aggressive energy. The old story of the man humiliated by his boss who comes home and beats his wife is actually a far more unusual occurrence than the opposite story: the man frustrated at home who comes to the office and "attacks" his work. Many women also have found that by having a job, or by creating specific work objectives in and around the home, they have an ideal way of "working off" the anger, rage, and frustration which may come from other sources.

A dynamic behind the need of many people to seek fraternal ties through work is the need to adapt to and defend against their unconscious competitive hostilities toward one another. The "boys" in the office, or in the fraternal professional society, are not only cooperating to ensure their mutual survival, they also may perceive their colleagues, on some level, as threats to their own individual survival. There is just so much room for each of us to be successful, for each of us to have his own secure territory. Work provides us with an outlet for our essentially ambivalent attitude to our fellow humans. We cooperate with each other for the common good and sublimate our innate hostilities toward our colleagues at the same time through socially acceptable competition.

The person who turns this aggressive facet of work into an

addiction is often superficially compliant and accommodating in his personal relationships out of a fear of rejection, retaliation, or a fear of the extent of his own hostilities. Instead of expressing his natural frustrations and anger at home, he displaces them by compulsively "attacking" and "wrestling" with his projects at work. A typical example is a fifty-one-year-old accountant who furiously "worked off " his inner rages at what he saw as his wife's coldness to him by being at his desk virtually around the clock all year. On a more subtle level, he enjoyed "breaking down" and reducing everything, people and things, into numbers.

Another example of the angry workaholic is the person who has had to "scratch and claw" completely on his own to make a success of himself. His comfortable but selfish parents gave him no support or encouragement, and his rage at them for this fuels his determination to succeed and show them up. He wants to be in a position to be able to refuse anything that they may belatedly want to give him. His anger is channeled into the joy of power, for which work is an endless resource.

2. THE ASHAMED WORK ADDICT

The discrepancy between the way a person is perceived and perceives himself at work and at home is a virtually universal phenomenon in all walks of life and work. Seeing an intimate friend at his or her workplace for the first time, or visiting the home of a fellow colleague, is almost always a revelation. Can the sweet, loving, mild-mannered woman next door really be the same person as this rather stern executive who seems so comfortable giving challenging assignments to her junior associates? The difference may be merely a function of her separate adaptations to the demands of each setting. Vastly different demands are made on us at work and in the personal realm. It is almost as if we can be different people in different situations. Intimacy is antithetical to the efficient goal-directedness of work, while formal structure, definition, linearity, efficiency, and productivity have no important place at home.

The fact that intimacy is usually absent in the workplace, and that our work interactions usually are characterized by greater distancing than we exercise in the personal realm, makes the work environment an ideal setting for fantasy gratification of all sorts. Personal reality need not be a distraction. It is in work situations that our daydreams of greatness and courage usually are played out. A person can be worshiped or unreservedly admired—popes, queens, presidents—only when the intimate details of their personal lives are not common knowledge. The greater the closeness, the less durable or monolithic the adoration. This truth does not apply only to those in high places. In general, we derive a much greater sense of unadulterated approval and acceptance at work, no matter what the job, than we do at home. No woman ever got a standing ovation from her husband or children, but many have basked in the glory of thunderous applause at testimonials for salesmanship or thirty years of service to their companies. Nobel prizes are given for great works, not for personal qualities. No matter what level a person may be at in his organization, he or she can be made to feel absolutely indispensable, and the gratification from this can nourish the wish to be deeply loved. It also provides people who otherwise feel ashamed or embarrassed about themselves with a means of relief from these distressing feelings.

The ashamed work addict is a person with low self-esteem. He is driven to extract recognition and approval from strict title hierarchies, salary grades, and superficial forms of respect in his corporate or other work environment, and this enables him to salvage some sense of self-worth. At home, he is just another member of the family, and his personal shame is reinforced by the absence of formal adulation and concrete respect. One thirty-eight-year-old banker, whose wife and children tried to love him but naturally did not show him the same level of deference as his secretary or associates, felt that his family didn't really care about him because they thought he was physically unattractive and a poor athlete. He was able to escape from these painful conclusions and sense of rejection by burying himself in his work at the office. In fact, his rejections were not from those in the present, but from his parents in the past, who much preferred an older brother, an extraordinary athlete, to him. His self-image was still stuck in these painful recollections from the past, and he compulsively used his work as a means of compensation for it.

3. The Competitive Work Addict

This is the person who uses work as a means of "scoring" the world and winning the game. Leisure activities and personal life, in which the strict measurement of comparative worth is not relevant, are avoided in favor of pursuits which can have numbers applied to them. His desire is to achieve bigger numbers than those he sees himself in competition with. This is a person who is always "proving himself," and the best way to do that is through work. Unlike the ashamed work addict, who seeks *love* that he feels he never had, the competitive work addict is seeking *respect*. If his mother rejected him, it was in favor of the stronger and bigger father, not the sibling. His mother may have loved him as a mother loves a child, but not as a woman loves a man. It is the thrill of victory, the taste of power, and the size of his achievement that drive this work addict. He is often someone, not surprisingly, who, as a child, unconsciously compared the size of his penis with his father's, and felt humiliated by the result. It may be a Freudian cliché by now that the boy child often attributes his mother's greater respect for the father to his large penis and consequent sexual prowess. But if this view remains unresolved into adulthood, intense competitive-ness continues. For many men, their work is their penis, and they desperately need to show that theirs is always bigger. One stockbroker succinctly opined: "You know what the stock market is? I'll tell you. It's a pecker contest, that's what!"

4. THE DEFENSIVE WORK ADDICT

Defense mechanisms are mental operations designed to protect us from unpleasant feelings, and work also functions effectively in this way. It enables us to *avoid* needs, desires, wishes, and feelings that may cause pain or distress. An illustration of how work enabled Albert Einstein to overcome the painful grief that followed his wife's death is contained in the following account:

"In 1936, Elsa lay dying even as Einstein and Banesh Hoffman and another physicist worked in Einstein's study. When she died, Hoffmann remembers Einstein looking haggard. They suggested their work be put off a few days. Einstein refused. 'Now, more than ever, I need my work,' he said."*

The ulteriorized quality of goal-directed work, where much of our mental activity is focused away from the present and on a symbolized objective in the future, protects us from feeling and sensation. Emotion is an experience of the present. Grief, mourning, feelings of rejection, unfulfilled sexual excitement, anxiety, shame, guilt, depression, and hostility can be warded off in the activity of goal-directed work. When we are working, we abstract ourselves mentally to some future state (where the goal resides), and, in doing so, we are not fully susceptible to the feelings of the present. This is the same process that we undertake when we daydream about being in

*William Stockton, "Celebrating Einstein," *New York Times Magazine,* Feb. 18, 1979.

a faraway place; we are projecting ourselves, not in time in this instance but in space.

By far the most effective way that work functions as a mechanism of defense is through the process of concentration. Concentration enables us to obliterate all other contents of the mind except that which is the focus of our attention. Fantasies, feelings, desires, wishes, needs, drives, and pain may be neutralized in the act of concentrating. Henry Ward Beecher once defined happiness as a mental state in which "a man is so busy that he does not know whether he is or is not happy.* For those who "bury" themselves in their work to avoid experiencing any sensation or feeling of distress or discomfort, anxiety or depression results once the defense—the work—comes to an end or is otherwise removed.

Unlike the other categories of work addiction, which are more chronic and characterological in nature, and which provide for the channeling of sexual or aggressive energy, defensive work compulsion is usually situational and time-limited, with the "binge" quality discussed earlier. Following the death of her husband of eighteen years, one patient immediately returned to work, and for six months did virtually nothing but paste-ups and mechanical drawings in a commercial art studio. She worked late into each evening, and every weekend. She avoided family and friends. As her weight began to drop markedly and her work suffered in quality, she felt the need for therapy. Slowly, she began to permit herself the process of mourning and grief which she had attempted to avoid, and her compulsive work behavior abated.

It should be emphasized here that *defense* is different from *escape*. A defense mechanism is a discrete mental process designed to alter specific painful mental content. Typical defenses, in addition to concentration and ulteriorization in

*Quoted in J. Cawelti, *Apostles of the Self-Made Man* (Chicago: University of Chicago Press, 1965).

work, are rationalization, intellectualization, projection, repression, and denial. Escape, on the other hand, is a nonspecific behavioral process. It is a taking flight *from* something (not necessarily *to* something), a leavetaking from a painful situation. Escapist reading, or other hobbies, may be mental forms of this behavior.

For some of us, work can be simply a flight from unpleasantness at home. Going to the office can be a great relief if being home involves trouble, tension, or conflict with one's spouse, children, neighbors, or parents. It does not mean that the person is going to be working when he is "at work," however. He has simply escaped the home for a safer, less troubling environment.

This escapist motivation may become compulsive and addictive in some people, but in that case it is an addiction more to escape than to work. The escapist *can* stop working without experiencing symptomatic distress as long as another escape is available.

One of my patients was married to a man with a chronic, progressively debilitating disease that caused increasing weakness and decay. He could not work and was cared for by a nurse at home; his wife became the sole support of the household. She found herself working double shifts during the week, and even on the weekend, to avoid seeing her husband's pathetic deterioration. Unlike most of the work addicts I have described in this chapter, she was entirely aware of what she was doing and why she was doing it. She did not particularly enjoy her work, but she was able to justify her eagerness to leave home for it because of the need to earn money for her husband's care. Anything else as convenient would have been just as satisfactory for this person to escape into, so it is not a particular aspect of the working process that drew her to it. For this reason, we cannot consider this a true addiction to work.

5. The Friendless, Lonely Work Addict

Work functions to bind people into larger groups, beyond the confines of the nuclear family unit, and gratifies our need to belong to a group of peers. The group recognizes and validates our productivity as an enhancement of its security and survival, and we are rewarded for our contributions by being assured of a place in this larger family. This need has its precursor in adolescence, when children begin to broaden the terms of primary allegiance from their parents to a group of peers.

The office setting, the factory, and the community of professional colleagues often provides an ideal outlet for the desires for fraternity. The "boys in the office," the employees in the bars after work, or the members of the usually work-related private clubs gather to satisfy group bonding needs, often with a common focus of antagonism to the parental figure of the "boss." Sometimes, antifeminine biases underlie this instinct in men and antimasculine feelings underlie it in women. In *The Gamesman*, Michael Maccoby describes a retreat for executives where the men are encouraged to urinate against the nearest redwood in the spirit of "old boy" openness, and where every year a play is produced in which men take women's roles. Women are roundly mocked and disdained.

The world of work has been a world dominated by men, a world in which women have been seen largely as accessories and not colleagues or rulers. This is undoubtedly changing swiftly, and, as it does, professional women's societies are springing up, not only to challenge exclusive male control of many areas in the world of work but to fulfill women's "fraternal" needs.

For the friendless, lonely work addict, it is not the process of working itself that is addictive. The feeling of acceptance in the community of other workers drives this person. The office society gives this work addict the illusion of friendships and family, but contact is rarely made outside of work. The superficial, formalized relationships on the job are all the intimacy these people can usually tolerate, and they long for opportunities to do extra work. Working overtime, evenings, weekends, and on vacations gives them a sense of belonging to a "team" that they enjoy nowhere else in their lives.

6. THE GUILTY WORK ADDICT

The ulterior quality of the working mind is the antithesis of a pleasurable immersion in immediate experience. We are abstracted, by our goal orientation, from the sensual to the mental. Even artists, if they are to work successfully at achieving their own defined objectives, must work ulteriorly. This gives rise to the common association of work with unpleasure. As essayist Alfred Polgar once said, "Work is what you do so that sometime you won't have to do it anymore."

The fact that we do not, in general, derive sensory pleasure from our work means that work can be available as an adaptive means of self-punishment and expiation of guilt. Many people who feel guilt, rational or irrational, may push themselves to work harder and harder, and the repudiation of pleasure that this represents does a great deal toward salving their consciences. Furthermore, the concentration and discipline of hard work are forms of aggression directed against the self, and easily lend themselves to sensations of personal flagellation.

In an experiment designed to test the association of hard work with guilt conducted by the General Electric Company, one group of hourly workers was systematically led to feel overpaid for their work, and their productivity was compared with a group which was led to feel fairly paid. The results clearly indicated that the people who felt overpaid had high levels of guilt, and this guilt translated into harder work and higher productivity than the control group demonstrated.*

Our criminal justice system often conceives of work as punishment. People convicted of crimes are often sentenced to work programs—and this does not necessarily mean twenty years of hard labor in a salt mine, or building a railroad in a chain gang. A doctor was sentenced to two years of medical service to the poor. Even though it may have been enjoyable, satisfying work for this particular man, it was still work, and as such it was deemed a proper way to pay for his crime. For an intensely guilt-ridden work addict, two years of leisure would probably have been a much greater punishment.

One of my patients was affected throughout his life by an unconscious feeling of guilt over the unfortunate death of his younger brother when he was four and the brother was one. He had played no role in his brother's death, which had been brought on by a congenital cardiac condition. But the normal sibling competitiveness of the jealous older boy toward the ill and much-fussed-over younger brother gave rise to typical childhood wishes that this unwelcome intruder in the domain he had "ruled" alone for three years would disappear or die. When the baby actually did die, the magical mind of the four-year-old implicated his unspoken wishes with the death of his brother.

This man dealt with his chronic, unresolved guilt by developing a variety of compulsive personality traits, including excessive neatness, orderliness, and frugality. He never wanted to experience any feelings that might evoke the loss he had endured at the sudden death of his brother. The other compulsive trait that he had developed was to become an extraordinarily hard worker at everything he set his mind to. He labored with punishing discipline and concentration, both

*The experiment is discussed in H. Levinson, *Executive Stress.*

at his personal life and at all tasks in his medical profession, a choice of career that undoubtedly had been influenced by his feelings about his brother's death. As they had for Barbara Williams (Chapter 9), work achievements gave him a sense of permanence, and a defense against the feelings associated with loss and death. But he also felt terribly guilty when he *wasn't* working. Hard work was a means of self-punishment for the "murder" of his brother. His guilt had stayed with him all his life, and it was "worked off" to some extent by his addictive work habits. And in his infinite agreeableness to take on any task, and to help out any other person with their work, he seemed, unconsciously, to be begging to be accepted as a "good" person, not a "bad" or hurtful one.

For the guilty work addict who needs to be punished, the more grueling the hours, the heavier the workload, the more these needs are met. One patient of mine was a man who had momentarily lost sight of his two-year-old daughter on a summer vacation as she was wandering dangerously close to the deep end of a swimming pool. He heard a splash and looked up, and she was under water. He dived in and brought her out, but she was already unconscious, and her lungs were filled with water. She was finally revived, but her development following this incident was inconsistent, and she later developed signs of minimal brain damage and certain learning disabilities. Her father knew that these problems very likely stemmed from the near-drowning and the period of oxygen deprivation.

His sense of guilt was enormous, but the damage was done, the clock could not be turned back, and there was no way that he could make up for his carelessness to his daughter. He could only assuage his guilt by inflicting punishment on himself, and this he did through his work. He was an attorney who drove himself ruthlessly. He was at his clients' mercy, working endlessly into nights and weekends to meet the requirements of his continuous influx of clients. One could say that he was merely avoiding having to go home and feel the guilt that seeing his daughter aroused in him. But there are many ways to stay away from home; he had to feel and acknowledge the sense of deserved punishment he got from his blistering work load. Furthermore, he eschewed most forms of potential self-congratulation from his work. He kept his fees low and did not compete for or accept honors or fame from within the legal community. He slept and ate poorly, and had had a coronary by the age of forty-five.

Another pathway to work addiction is through sexual guilt and shame. People who are threatened and made anxious by any intimations of lusty fantasy or sensation are infinitely more comfortable in the sexually neutralized arena of work. This does not only apply to fear of sex in the traditional sense of lovemaking or intercourse. One patient of mine was made very tense whenever she had to buy clothing for herself. She could not acknowledge that she had any "sensual" reaction to style, texture, or color in clothing or furnishings. She preferred "drab." She was a person who self-protectively had to renounce all sexual and sensory "appetites" ever since infancy, when her mother showed very inconsistent responses to her earliest feeding needs. Other people directly renounce sexual or sexually derived desires following Oedipal stirrings, when guilt over lusty fantasies for the opposite-sex parent arises from the clear prohibitions of that period. Where masturbation is rigidly forbidden in childhood, we can often expect a sexually repressed adulthood in which work may become the dominating outlet for gratification of all sorts.

7. The Latent Homosexual Work Addict

This particular dynamic takes two general forms in men. In the first, the man with unconscious homosexual wishes to be dominated by another man draws gratification from work which keeps him in a continually submissive position with powerful bosses and clients. He may complain interminably about being violated by their demands on him, but he never fails to oblige.*

Some men with unconscious homosexual desires undo them by being "hypermasculine" in their work. They are abrasive, driven, competitive, arbitrary, impolite, and excessively aggressive. They have a need to prove how much they are "real" men—more to themselves, unfortunately, than to anyone else.

8. The Narcissistic Work Addict

(See Chapter 12).

9. The Obsessive Work Addict

The drive to categorize, organize, and define becomes all-controlling for some of us, and leads to perfectionism and pathological orderliness. Such people are intensely fearful of vagueness and sloppiness, as if their very sanity depended on precision and neatness. One patient had to "know" if a certain man loved her or didn't love her. Positive impressions were not good enough; she had to know exactly how love was defined, and then "prove" if his behavior conformed to the definition she sought. For her, it was as if life were something that could be played out merely with a dictionary or a rule book. She had to keep her mind as neat as her hairdo, and she panicked if something in either area was out of place. She admitted that she felt she could easily go insane if neatness and orderliness eluded her. The only way she could square this need with reality was to live an extremely restricted

*For a very detailed study of the homosexual dynamic in a case of work addiction, see the paper of Kramer listed in the Bibliography.

loner's life in a studio apartment with a bare minimum of possessions. She worked as a bookkeeper, adding and "proofing" columns of figures day in and day out. Her obsessiveness and her procrastination about the man who professed to love her soon ended his interest in her, much to her relief.

This was a woman for whom the need to know "where she stood" at all times took precedence over virtually all other values in her life. Other people express this need in a variety of ways. Some are forever adding up their bank balances to give them a sense of security. Others must refer to their projects lists for structure, definition, and the feeling of order.

Still other obsessive work addicts reveal their compulsion by insisting on doing everything themselves. One of my patients, the successful president of a firm employing two hundred people, refused for years to employ either a secretary or a personnel manager. He answered all his own phone calls, personally interviewed all job applicants from mail-room personnel to vice-presidents, and handwrote all his memoranda. He also "worked things to death" before he could consider them finished. Everything had to be "perfect," to resemble exactly the mental image of his previsualized goal. As a result of his compulsion for effectiveness and control, he was terribly inefficient. He worked until two every morning, and would rise before seven. He had great difficulty saying that anything was ever finished.

Only those activities which have a clear beginning and end can satisfy the obsessive work addict. Leisure is too free-floating for this person. The emphasis in leisure time is not on getting things "finished." Only in work, where precise goals define structures with a clear, linear organization, can an obsessive work addict relax and feel "complete." The home-maker who tries to make her household into a static showpiece and her children into obedient toy soldiers falls into this category.

10. The Passive-Dependent Work Addict

People with strong aggressive needs for personal definition
and a sense of mastery thrive on the beginning and end of the
work process: the initiatory or goal-setting phase and the
achievement phase. Although the middle phase of a work task
can gratify the aggressive individual who enjoys "grappling
and wrestling" with a challenge, it can also provide more
passive and dependent people with their satisfactions as well.
These are people who want to be taken care of and to be told
what to do, who want to carry something through once it is
set in motion by someone else, and who prefer to let another
person take the bows at the end.

Many people eschew initiative in work but fit right into
procedures and rules prescribed by others in authority. They
are comfortable with the routines and organization that work
imposes, in contrast to the vagueness and diffuseness of
"personal time." They initiate nothing in work that is a
reflection of their own singular tastes and inclinations. They
eat what is served in the company cafeteria, and never have to
ask what they themselves like. Their clothing is rigidly
dictated by the "uniform" they perceive as required for their
particular job. They are at home with the "necessity" of work,
and relieved at not having to make choices. They are infinitely
"agreeable" in their nonworking lives, in order to avoid any
personal responsibility or commitment.

In addition to the authority naturally imposed by organizational structure, authority also comes from work goals
themselves. There are known, time-proven methods which a
worker must apply to reach defined goals. I am not referring
only to line workers in a factory or the other blue-collar
employees. Even at the highest levels of management or in
professional activities, it is typical to find little continuous
personal initiative and creative establishment of long-range

goals. A doctor, for example, waits for patients to come to him or her with their problems. They define his task for him, and prelearned techniques can be set in motion—in many cases, quite routinely and automatically. Surely, some discretion must be used and decisions made in the middle phase of work, but it does not compare with the degree of initiative associated with the primary establishment of original creative goals, such as developing new products, creating new markets, or formulating a whole new form of treatment of an illness.

The sorts of workers who relish the middle phase of work exclusively, who prefer administration to creative planning, are often people who have great difficulty in their personal lives. In the personal sphere, considerable initiative is important if we are to be successful. We need to define and identify our tastes: which movies we want to see, what kind of food we prefer, which friends to invite to dinner, how to decorate our homes, where to live, what we desire for our children, and where to go on vacation. We cannot simply take orders or rely on impersonal authority to give us direction. This problem underlies one of the paradoxes of people who "love" their work but who feel lost and alienated at home. They are often people whose work *leads* them, and in situations where they must come forth with personal preferences which affirm their own unique identities, they are at sea.

A patient of mine who happened to be a physician was addicted to amphetamines—but only, it seemed, on weekends and vacations. His work gave him the "push" he needed during the week, but he lacked sufficient self-definition or desire on weekends to take initiative and identify what he wanted to do. He took amphetamines to give him the strength for this. His wife found him infuriating, because he always deferred to her wishes. He rationalized that he was simply being accommodating and kind. Actually, he was lost.

Another patient, who had some insight into his needs to

hide behind or within other people, had this to say: "I feel like an acorn sometimes. I have to decide if I'm going to become squirrel food or a mighty oak. To my way of thinking, the squirrel-food route has a lot of merit. As an oak tree, you're out there all alone, buffeted by wind, snow, rain, and bird shit. Sure, you can be admired for your majesty and power. But I'll trade that for the warm comfort inside the belly of the squirrel."

This was a man who had experienced a disturbingly chaotic childhood. His alcoholic and promiscuous mother, who bore him out of wedlock, was unavailable to him for years at a time. His father was unknown to him, and probably even to his mother. He went the route from orphanages to multiple foster homes, and he longed all his life for secure, reliable maternal comforting. He found some degree of it in his work as a desk clerk in a big hotel. He abided by accepted procedures and was extremely hard-working, putting in whole extra shifts of overtime several times a week. The very fact that there was no sense of personal achievement associated with this kind of work was ideal for him. He rejected a need for publicly visible personal identity. Shame over being a "bastard" pervaded his psyche, and he refused even to register to vote or to apply for a passport, a driver's license, or even a telephone number. He received his mail at a post-office box.

This man was extremely bright and gifted. He had written several novels and short stories, but they never left his apartment. He was terrified at the idea of becoming published, of having a public identity and having to assume the responsibilities that would accompany that. Interestingly enough, he came to me for treatment of sexual impotence. He was highly moralistic about "recreational sex" (through which he was conceived), and feared the mastery role that an erect penis would put him into.

11. The Pre- or Post-Psychotic Work Addict

There are a great many disturbed individuals who function with dramatic effectiveness in the highly defined and structured world of work. Once they leave work, they lose their bearings, and they become enormously disoriented and anxious. The worlds of intimate personal relationships and leisure are too vague and diffuse for them, and their precarious senses of self are too easily shattered without external supports.

Such symptoms as depersonalization and derealization may occur. The patient does not feel that his or her own body or self is "real." In depersonalization, physical boundaries are diffuse, and the person is bewildered by not knowing if he is inside his own body or someone else's. In derealization, there are defects in one's sense of the reality of the external world. Nothing seems connected to a framework, a meaningful order, or a simple relation of cause and effect. Time loses its structure. One woman patient, a schoolteacher, was hospitalized for four successive summers during her "vacations." Without the clear landmarks her job provided for defining her self and her environment, she became psychotic. At four o'clock, she panicked because she didn't know if it was four a.m. or four p.m. The letters became meaningless sounds. She was disoriented even to her own name, which also began to sound unreal to her.

This woman was dreadfully afraid of reading a good novel and "getting lost in it." Putting the book down and reorienting her consciousness to her real surroundings would sometimes be very difficult, for she didn't seem to know if she was still in the book or elsewhere, where she always felt unfamiliar. A paranoid delusion, the belief that she was being followed by Russian KGB spies, emerged as a kind of organizing preoccupation which brought order to her mental chaos. This is the way that delusions function. They are primitive "beliefs" which simplify and give "meaning" to events which themselves would be terrifyingly disconnected. With the delusion, the psychotic feels that he or she "understands," and the panic of disorientation is diminished.

For this woman, it was clear that she could not tolerate a three-month vacation from her job. The withdrawal symptoms were far too debilitating. She realized that she had to work a summer job from virtually the moment her regular school year ended until it began again in the fall. She sought my help about three years before her mandatory retirement age. Therapy consisted of some analysis of her total dependency on work for psychic stability, but by far the most important task for this woman, whose age and degree of pathology militated against efforts for substantial personality changes, was to establish a clear "occupational" structure for her retirement years.

12. The Sexually Frustrated or Impotent Work Addict

Many people derive their greatest sexual satisfaction from fantasies encouraged in the workplace. Flirtations are commonplace. Men may excite themselves with signs of *macho* triumphs that would be absurdly undermined by greater intimacy. In fact, many men have asked their female colleagues for dates and then been surprised when they are rejected. They do not expect the rejection because they do not understand the formalized nature of relationships at work. Flirtations occur *between roles*, not necessarily *between the people in the roles*.

Normal voyeuristic and exhibitionistic needs, conscious and unconscious, are frequently gratified in the setting of work, where formal distancing of relationships provides firm limits to acting on sexual impulses. Exhibitionism, showing off, is protected by the strict rules and roles in the office. In a paper entitled "Psychodynamics of Sexual Humor: The Secretary," the following joke is recounted: "For many years, a wealthy businessman had been mercilessly teased by his seductive but unattainable secretary. In avowing his passion for her, he continually promised, 'I'll remember you in my will.' Upon his death, Miss Jones, the secretary, sat at the reading of the will, waiting to reap her harvest. The lawyer read: 'And for my beautiful but uncooperative secretary, whom I avowed to remember in my will: Hi there, Miss Jones!' "

The only redeeming feature of this horrible joke is what it reveals about the dynamics of exhibitionism and voyeurism in the office. The fact that the businessman would tolerate the "mercilessness" of his inappropriately seductive secretary for so many years suggests that gratification of his voyeurism was more important to him than the realization of intimate sexual relations with an attractive secretary. If realizing his desires had been important to him, he could have fired Miss Jones and replaced her with a more accommodating woman. In the same vein, Miss Jones was enjoying unrestricted exhibitionism. In the office, work productivity is the overriding value, not the quality of personal interactions or character traits. If Miss Jones did her job very well, that is what counted in the end, and her exhibitionism was protected and tolerated.

Sexually impotent men may enjoy fantasies of conquest from flirtations which are permitted and fostered in the work environment. They flee from the failures in their personal lives to the formalized pseudo-intimacy of the office, where their sexual performance is unknown, but where they can get continued reinforcement for their "potential." They are protected from exposure to failure by the rationalized prohibitions against mixing business and pleasure.

The sexually frustrated woman may, correspondingly,

enjoy fantasied "affairs" with men at work, where flirtations, or even normal courtesies to a co-worker, may be actively misinterpreted and relished as signs of deeper affection. If actual affairs do occur, they are often viable only as work-related liaisons, in which true intimacy is warded off by the strictures of the work relationship. Distance is usually further assured by the married status of the man.

One of my patients was a sixty-two-year-old unmarried woman who had been the personal secretary of a particular executive for thirty-five years. Their interaction was strictly limited to business tasks at hand, and they addressed one another only as "Mr. Green" and "Miss Brown." She was referred to me in a state of profound depression after the executive was transferred overseas to run his company's foreign office. It was as if she had lost a lover. For thirty-five years, this woman had secretly maintained a fantasied affair with her boss, an affair which never had to be challenged by realistic intimacy. It sustained her and even seemed to gratify her deepest sexual needs. He made her feel important, significant, indispensable, and even loved, through the kinds of formal statements that would never apply to any personal relationships outside an office setting. She had saved and cherished a yellowed copy of his first memo to his own boss requesting a raise in her pay. In it he praised her work and character glowingly, but in terms and in a format that a husband or a lover would never have any reason to use toward his loved one.

One further way that work provides an outlet for sexual discharge is associated with the fact that all work has not only a goal, but a climax. There are some people who are addicted to the sheer suspense and excitement of work. Anxiety and sexual excitement are close cousins, because they both involve the anticipation of a future event. "Will we make the deadline?" "Will the jury say 'not guilty'?" "Will we close the deal?" One cannot underestimate the subtle erotic potential of goal-oriented (or climax-oriented) work.

Some people try to prolong the "foreplay" phase of work and attempt to defer final achievement. They are excited by the mounting tension as deadlines appear, but, in self-destructive ways, they undermine the successful accomplishment that would signal the end of the buildup and the excitement. One journalist I treated would endlessly work and rework a story, often mangling it while dueling with deadlines, and frequently miss them in the process. His problem was not so much procrastination or lack of self-confidence, but an unconscious desire to create and sustain a continuous "thriller" of his life. For him, achievement and success would seem humdrum and boring.

12

Work and Narcissism

Sexual feelings can sometimes be directly expressed toward the materials of our work, and many people experience a kind of erotic attachment to them and to their completed products. This may occur not only in the creative arts, where the senses are deliberately aroused and excited. I know of a stockbroker, for example, who saved all the superfluous records of his most profitable transactions and glowed with an intensely sexualized sense of fulfillment when he took them out and read them through. He would sit at his desk and visually caress a sheet of paper that showed the sale of a stock he had bought years before "for peanuts" and had sold at the top of the market.

In *The Story of a Novel*, Thomas Wolfe described the euphoric moment when he signed his first contract and received his first advance in this way: "I left the publisher's office that day and entered into the great swarm of men and women who passed constantly along Fifth Avenue at 48th Street, and presently I found myself at 110th Street, and from that day to this I have never known how I got there." In a letter, he described how he walked for days with his contract and advance check tucked into his inner breast pocket: "There is literally no reason why I should walk around New York with these documents, but in a busy crowd I will sometimes take them out, gaze tenderly at them, and kiss them passionately."

These examples are good illustrations of a variety of sexual expression that we call narcissism. I am presenting a discussion of narcissism and narcissistic work addiction in this separate chapter because of the timeliness of the concept and the need to distinguish between normal and excessive degrees of narcissism. Christopher Lasch has asked, in his extremely challenging book, (see Bibliography), if we are becoming a culture of narcissists. Indeed, as he illustrates, there is much evidence for the contention that emphasis on self and self-development continues to be an overwhelming element in mid-twentieth century Western culture. Identifying the social factors which may give rise to this is beyond the scope of this book. But a discussion of the psychological dimension of narcissism, and the role of work in narcissism, is something that I do want to concentrate on here.

Narcissus, a character in Greek mythology, fell in love with his own reflection. In the sense that our achievements are symbolic representations of our selves, loving our own work creations is similar to Narcissus' particular passion. Our work products are an image of ourselves in somewhat the same way that our reflection in the mirror is. Narcissism, in moderation, is normal, and basic to the development of self-respect. We ought to love our images in the mirror as we ought to love ourselves in our works. We all have narcissistic needs.

Female narcissism has traditionally been associated with physical beauty, not with work achievement. Clothing, adornments, jewelry, and perfumes to enhance personal physical attractiveness have been, for better or for worse, a major element in the normal narcissism of women. Men's characteristic investment in the realm of goal-directed works leads to a brand of narcissism associated with accomplishments of power, endurance, courage, bravery, and relationships which range beyond the home. No doubt there have always been exceptions to this, and there is also no doubt that the balance in male-female narcissism is changing. Male plumage is coming back into vogue, more men are becoming "mothers," and more and more women are finding themselves admired for their exploits of power and worldly achievement.

But narcissism, or self-love, must be distinguished from other forms of love. In the development of sexual loving from infantile to mature forms, the objects of our sexual drives evolve from the more controllable to the less controllable. Freud delineated stages of sexual development from the narcissistic, autoerotic phase to that of interpersonal genital love. The immature expression of the sexual instinct focuses on objects which are controllable, situations in which only a wish may, magically, be sufficient to establish gratification.

The infant is in quite commanding control of its mother's nipple and of parts of its own body for sensory fulfillment. In more mature forms of love between people, the control of the loved object—not simply a body part, but a whole other person—is much less certain and not even so desirable. Mature love objects have lives of their own; they do not respond automatically, as a mother or our own genitals do, to gratify our every wish. Mutual respect for each other's autonomy and independence, compromise, harmony, and rapport come only from the highly complex working through of a mature, dynamic, giving relationship.

People who "love their work" exclusively, more than they can love other people, who treat work materials and products as kinds of "sex objects," are usually people who are unable to love what they cannot control. Work materials and the process of work itself can be subject to the expression of loving, giving feelings, but this attachment is often associated with the need to control and manipulate the source of gratification, to take from it without giving to it. Personal and family relationships are clearly not as accessible to the mastery drive as paints, theories, bricks, law briefs, insurance policies, manuscripts, surgical techniques, sales receipts, and publishers' contracts.

As an outlet for constructive aggression, and the creative accomplishment of objectives which define and fortify our personalities, work can reach the most advanced heights of human potential. As an exclusive outlet for sexual love, however, it represents an expression of narcissistic sexuality. In narcissism, mutuality and "loss of self" in the loved object and the relinquishment of the need to control, which characterize mature loving, are repudiated in favor of domination, mastery, and self-satisfaction.

The legitimate gratifications of control are captured in the words of a contributor to *Working It Out*, a fine collection by and about women and their work. Comparing scholarly work to mothering, historian Kay Keeshan Hamod writes: "I love scholarly work, because you *force* it into shape. It's not like sitting around for nine months, waiting for something to happen to you." Mothering in many ways is an assault on a person's narcissism. The mother is not applauded for her work, as she may be for a fine scholarly manuscript; more often, she is yelled at, abruptly awakened, urinated on, and reduced to cleaning up vomit and spilled cereal. Mothering is, ideally, a giving role, not a taking role. This is not to say, however, that mothers cannot be extremely narcissistic with their friends, their clothes, their husbands, their homes, and even their children. Their behavior may be geared in the extreme toward drawing attention to themselves. They may take their children's achievements for their own, aggrandizing all that belongs to them through manipulation of separation anxiety and guilt. Narcissistic mothers may keep their children close by, overdramatizing the hostility and insecurity of the outside world and making the child feel guiltily obligated to its mother because of "all I've done for you."

Narcissism thrives on appreciation and verification of self-worth from others. But where love of work, as a form of self-love, is the *exclusive* outlet for the sexual drive, it can be seen as a kind of masturbation, a pathological narcissism.* Masturbatory love begins and ends with the self. If it is a form of giving, only the self benefits from it.

In some people the urge to work is truly an urge which stems from the empathic, giving quality of the sexual drive. For them, work *is* love. It enables them to help and serve selflessly, whether it is to fulfill the needs of their families or the needs of the larger communities of which they are a part. The aggressive satisfaction that stems from the achievement of personally conceived goals is subordinated to the pleasure derived from fulfilling the needs of others. Such people are rare; usually they are employed in the "helping" professions: teaching, nursing, the clergy, medicine, and social work. The ability to give and to serve others is the foundation of their self-esteem.

Narcissistic work addicts are people whose early life experiences have given rise to deep personal insecurity, and who compulsively depend on work to compensate for the otherwise unremitting sense of inadequacy they unconsciously feel about themselves.

One highly successful forty-two-year-old insurance executive described how, for him, lovemaking had always been a performance to be measured and graded. His attention inevitably was on the ultimate orgasms he and his partner would experience, on whether they would be simultaneous and intense or disconnected and weak. He failed to enjoy any loving harmony from a sexual union. He couldn't simply *be* in

---

*See Kernberg, *Borderline Conditions and Pathological Narcissism*, for a complete discussion of clinical narcissism.

the present; he always had to be thinking ahead. Driven to adopt a working frame of mind in all situations, he was methodical and systematic in the aggressive pursuit of his sexual goals. This frame of mind was certainly adaptive and effective at his office, but it was far from ideal in a loving embrace. The unconscious fear of the loss of personal boundaries in a loving intimacy was behind this man's work compulsion. Tangible accomplishment of defined goals enhanced his sense of identity. He *was* his successes, and *only* his successes. Love, empathy, or giving of any sort threatened this identity.

Most of the people in the work-addict categories described in the last chapter come to the attention of a psychiatrist because of their own subjective sense that "something is wrong" in their work habits. They are aware of the distress they experience when work ceases, and they know on some level that their behavior does not represent simply a deep love for the process and content of work. They feel that their relationships with others, which they care more or less deeply about, are impaired and interfered with by their compulsion to work. They are able to be critical of themselves, and to realize that their own happiness is affected by factors in themselves which seem uncontrollable. They will usually come for help on their own.

The narcissistic work addict, however, almost never seeks help from purely internal motivation. He or she claims to feel perfectly happy, and problems arise only because other people in their lives cannot or will not adjust to them. Such a person may be married, be affable and well liked, have a big family and a large group of friends, and work in a sizable organization with many people, but he is, in his heart, a loner. To him (although he would consciously deny this), relationships with other people should lead only to gratification of *his* needs; otherwise they are frustrating and must be avoided. There is rarely any tolerance for "give and take" in such a person. Although it may not be apparent at first glance, there is usually only "take."

The self-centeredness in this person is a primary attribute, even when he is presumably "giving." His concern that his wife and children always "have the best," that his wife be satisfied in lovemaking with a terrific orgasm,* or that his community is well served by his efforts are, in the end, concerns about the quality of his performance and how much approval he will get. He is not competitive in the strict sense of the word, because being "better" than someone else is never good enough. He must be "the best," "the only one," or absolutely "perfect." If he gets the best performance evaluation of all his co-workers, but the slightest criticism is suggested in it, he becomes obsessed with that "flaw" and becomes either vindictive or depressed.

Beneath this independent, individualistic facade is the feeling that if he needs help, he is showing weakness and dependency, qualities which he is compelled—because the unconscious desire *to be dependent* is actually so strong—to disavow completely. He pays his bills as soon as he receives them, and is proud never to be in anyone's debt. He certainly never asks for favors. In addition to the need to deny dependency wishes, his "rugged individualism" camouflages a deep-seated fear of rejection should he broadcast a need—a fear of reexperiencing the feeling of rejection which marked his early childhood.

The narcissistic work addict is preoccupied, consciously or unconsciously, with control. He finds it intolerable when his children don't finish what is on their plates. "Idle conversation" makes him impatient because it doesn't lead to productive work. The narcissistic work addict prefers working early in the morning, during lunch hours, or late in the evening

*For a discussion of this specific concern see the paper by Clifford listed in the Bibliography.

when he can be alone, when other people are not around to "bother" him. He often must travel two hours by train to his office, but rarely minds this because of the uninterrupted reading or work that can be done during these four hours a day. When he gets home, there is rarely time to do more than eat quickly and go to sleep. And his sleep may be interrupted several times so that he may pursue a work-related idea which inspired him during the night.

For this kind of narcissist, work means everything. Work is the arena of control, and this is his most fundamental need. He can relate only to things he can command, and things which bolster his sense of self. Intimacy, sharing, empathy, and easygoing "give and take" actually frighten him (although, again, he would never admit it), because they represent a relinquishing of control. He feels depleted by any form of giving, as if the boundaries of his self would come apart. This may give his character a somewhat paranoid quality: "What do you want from me?" and "Why do people always take, take, take?" are common refrains from the narcissist. He may appear sometimes to be hostile or arrogant, but this actually is not the case. What looks like hostility (which would in fact be a healthier, more highly developed reaction) is actually a lack of awareness of other people. The narcissist is fixated at an egocentric stage of psychological growth in which one's own needs dominate one's consciousness, and in which there is a blindness for, or lack of interest in, the nuances of interpersonal relationships and the needs of others. He lives in a world of mirrors, without windows.

Some narcissistic people appear superficially to be extremely caring about the feelings of people around them who are upset. One woman tells about her husband, who reacts almost volcanically whenever she mentions even the slightest feeling of distress. When she is happy, however, he ignores her. He cannot tolerate the presence of distress in his wife, because for him, this means that she is paying some attention to herself and is not completely available to him. He immediately tries to "do something about it"; he is unable to simply listen and empathize. In fact, in his effort to restore her availability to him, he turns her discomfort or sadness into a work project for himself.

In his need to work on things, the narcissistic work addict cannot have conversations about "small things." Topics for discussion should represent challenges, and should focus on large events which require serious thought and extensive information. Simply talking about trivia, about what the kids did in school or the fact that the neighbors are getting divorced, makes this person edgy. One such man's idea of dinner-table conversation was to quiz everyone about the day's articles in *The New York Times*.

(I have been using the male pronoun to describe the narcissistic work addict, but it should not obliterate the fact that women as well as men can demonstrate these personality traits.)

As a creature of the aggressive instinct, this kind of work addict does not understand that the essence of personal relationships is not control and victory, but rather "keeping the ball in play." This tennis metaphor was given by a man who complained about the way his wife played tennis with him. She didn't enjoy a good rally at all, but played every point to win. Unfortunately, she behaved the same way at a dinner party or at home in the living room. In her work, this was adaptive. She was successful in an environment which was geared to mastery and the accomplishment of objectives, and which fed her need for personal glory. She derived little pleasure from the personal interactions in her work that led to her achievements. When the family rode for six hours to a ski resort, she read annual reports, because, as she put it, "What can you talk about with your husband and kids for that long that's productive?" She was basically a salesperson in her work, and she was thrilled with every new sale that she made.

But once a sale was accomplished, she had no interest whatsoever in servicing her customers, or even in staying in contact with them. She couldn't stop to savor the taste of the victory, because she had to start moving immediately toward the next one.

A vignette about the way this couple planned a vacation illustrates an aspect of their problem. The wife would say, "Where do you want to go on a vacation this year?" The husband would bring home brochures, books, and magazine articles and would start to look forward to spending an evening with her going over these materials. Half the fun of a vacation for him was in spending time with his wife making plans together. The actual decision and the ultimate vacation itself were almost secondary. She, on the other hand, was exceedingly businesslike: "Let's just make a decision about where to go, make reservations, and be done with it." To her, the objective of making a decision about the vacation was primary, and she wanted to take the shortest, quickest route to it. She felt no need to waste time playing out different alternatives with him. She had other more important things to do.

This woman was the same way about eating and having arguments. A sensuously slow meal with a good bottle of wine, an experience in which all the tastes are savored without regard to the clock, was a negative prospect for her. Nor could she understand how an argument could be seen as a more loving act than a quick truce. Whereas her husband perceived it as an earnest attempt to maintain communication and iron out differences, to her an argument was simply a "hassle." She always wanted to impose a compromise and be done with it. "Why waste two hours coming to a decision that could be made in five minutes?"

The narcissistic work addict comes to his or her addiction from a deep unconscious sense of personal insecurity. He needs work as a source of continual reinforcement and bolstering for a weak, inadequate sense of self. Leisuring, the experience of "losing" oneself in sensation, of expanding or dissolving the boundaries of the self in communion with nature, works of art, a good meal, or other people, is frightening. He has built his personality around the anticipation of rejection, loss, or other catastrophe, and feels he cannot let his guard down to enjoy anything in the present. Like the third little pig in the children's story who knows the wolf is always about, he has built walls of bricks around himself. He fears that if he is not vigilant, if he permits himself to love and to give, he will deplete himself irreparably and not be able to reconstitute his sense of identity and definition.

His reluctance, or fear, of giving can show itself in ways which are puzzling at first glance. When I began to treat people of considerable wealth who had great difficulty spending money on material things which they could easily afford and enjoy, I found it perplexing. How could a man worth several million dollars be satisfied to live in a furnished studio apartment, listen to music on an old portable radio, and wear suits which were at least ten years old? All money this man earned went back into his ever-expanding stock portfolio. Other cases were not so extreme, but difficulty spending money on themselves was present in many people who had plenty of it to spend. If they had to, they could always spend it far more easily on others (who would show appreciation) than on themselves. They hated to go shopping, and often they procrastinated on plans for a vacation or the purchase of a new house until it was too late.

Several factors have become clear about these people, whose problems all revolve around the idea of "giving." To buy expensive clothes or a fine stereo system means to spend money. The narcissist regrets the expenditure, the departure of his money, more deeply than he appreciates the clothing or the music. Although he doesn't want to give anything to get them, he will accept something if it is given to him. The gift means that someone sees that he needs it and shows concern for him. Often, though, he doesn't want to have to take care of anything once he gets it. Any possession requires care and attention; he would rather have junk that requires no maintenance. Also, the more opulent he appears, the less people will sympathize with him and want to take care of him. In fact, the large discrepancy between his wealth and his threadbare appearance makes him more pathetic and in greater apparent need. This forces his wife or friend to buy all his clothes for him, like a mother. By putting his money back into the stock market, he feels that he has to give nothing to get more money. What he has begets by itself. It sits there and earns for him.

One patient told me that he was afraid to love his possessions, natural beauty, or other people because of a feeling that if he let himself love something or someone, he might want them "too much." By "too much" he meant that loving and attachment would make him vulnerable to disappointment and rejection. This statement expressed an awareness that his neediness ran so deep that he was afraid that he might go overboard if he permitted himself to like anything except his work. Otherwise, he would lose control of himself, lose a sense of proportion and reality. His work kept his desires in check. It also provided him with gratifications that he had a fair chance of controlling. Loving a person, we take much more of a chance, and risk failure more, than if we limit our "loving," say, to arguing cases before juries. There, if we do our homework, if we "learn our lines," we are surer of being successful. In personal relationships, learning techniques, strategies, and playing roles can only get us so far.

There are two prototypical early-childhood experiences which give rise to narcissistic work addiction. In the first scenario, the child gets "too little"; in the second, the child gets "too much." The products of both situations are extremely insecure, and both become compulsively attached to working—but they express their insecurities in different ways.

The work addict who got "too little" is someone who perceived his childhood (consciously or unconsciously) as cold, devoid of spontaneous affection, and replete with important losses—the death of parents or siblings, frequent family moves and consequent loss of friends, parental illness and hospitalization, and the like. He remembers feelings of emotional deprivation and frequent painful rejections. The mothers of these people were often depressed during the postpartum period and beyond, anxiety-ridden, or characteristically self-centered. Feeding problems were common in childhood, largely because of the mother's insensitivity to the child's needs. Thumb-sucking and a longer than normal attachment to the threadbare "security blanket" were common ways the child had of providing himself with the illusion of a soothing, reliable, always available mother.

The deprivation felt by these people may be entirely in fantasy, as is the case of many individuals who were adopted in infancy. Their childhoods may have been enormously secure and gratifying, but the lingering sense of having been abandoned and rejected by their natural mother creates an inner void which, often, can never seem to be filled. One such patient had a nightly dream, long into adulthood, in which she saw herself being dropped out of an airplane, landing in a shambles on the ground.

People with this perception of childhood don't always become narcissistic work addicts. They may express their neediness in many different ways, some of which culminate in work *paralysis* and *direct* dependency on others. Work addicts, on the other hand, express their dependency *indirectly*. The thrill of completed work, for them, is the gratification which originates in the desire to be nursed and completely satisfied.

They want to feel "full," to have something to "hold onto," and their work is their security blanket.

Professor Abraham Zaleznik, of Harvard Business School, described the tragic case of James Forrestal, the first U.S. Secretary of Defense, in an article entitled "Management of Disappointment." Forrestal turned to work addiction, first on Wall Street, then in government, as the ultimate outcome of a harsh mother-child relationship. "As the result of a complex psychological process, the individual renounces nurturance and other tender emotional exchanges, and substitutes instead a burning ambition and drive to achieve. If the individual has the ability, as Forrestal clearly had in abundance, he may achieve leadership and success . . . but he is vulnerable to continuing disappointment that may lead to breakdown."* In Forrestal's case, he committed suicide after being replaced by President Truman as Defense Secretary.

Many maternally deprived people, however, may not be especially ambitious or aggressive in their work aspirations. They just like a lot of work. We find them often at the middle levels of organizations, secure in their niches, comforted by the intrinsic gratifications of the work itself and by the praise and approval which come from the people around them.

The work addicts who got "too little" as children do not generally become private entrepreneurs. Most cases of ambitious, aggressive, independent, entrepreneurial workers have had "too much" mothering rather than too little. These people have memories of smothering closeness to their parents, feelings of having been controlled, manipulated, and overly protected by parents who seemed to need their children as much as or more than the children needed them. The developmental phase during which these people were most sensitized is the "anal" phase, when autonomy and self-

*A. Zaleznik, "Management of Disappointment," in *Stress, Success, and Survival* (Cambridge, Mass.: Harvard Business Review, 1979).

control are first emphasized. Toilet training was frequently overdramatized in these cases, and the child comes away from the experience with needs to protect himself from his parents' assault on his body. As a result, his personality crystallizes around the need to be free of external control, to be in charge, to depend on no one. He is more overtly angry and explosive than the "orally deprived" work addict, who is afraid of biting any hand that might feed him. Where the "too little" type is usually orderly, neat, punctual, and thrifty (he holds onto whatever he has for dear life), the "too much" addict can be disorganized, keep people waiting with relish, be unpredictable, and spend money in great bursts of extravagance. In a sense, he, too, has been rejected by his parents. The subtle message he has gotten from them is that he counts for nothing without them, that he cannot "make it" (note the anal connotation) on his own. His reaction is to say, "I'll show them!" He lusts after signs of personal achievement and self-definition, but he gives credit to no one but himself. Where the "deprived" work addict is usually most comfortable in the middle phase of work, drawing upon others in authority for direction and guidance, the "overprotected" addict delights in initiation and achievement. He can delegate work more easily, and he doesn't mind letting others implement his creative ideas as long as *he* gets the credit.

13

The Fear of Success

We all know people who have great difficulty succeeding or achieving anything of significance in their work, or who may succeed and be very productive but always seem to be fighting against something in themselves in the process. Of course, one of the most common reasons for this is simple lack of interest in the jobs which may be available to an individual. Work which is neither challenging, pleasurable, nor meaningful is going to make for uninspired or unmotivated workers.

But there are many people who are endowed with considerable intelligence and imagination and have unlimited access to whatever field of endeavor they consciously want to be in, but cannot live up to their potential or suffer when they do. Their psyches, not the vicissitudes of the job market, seem to be the primary determinants in their lack of success. Someone once said to me, "Every good thing I've ever done in my life has been followed by a migraine headache." He could succeed, but suffered terribly whenever he did.

Fear of success is the most significant dynamic factor underlying work inhibition. We are able to identify an extreme group of success-phobic people who, in their virtual work paralyses, appear to be helplessly dominated by their own needs to merge and fuse with others, and who are intensely threatened by the isolation and disconnectedness of self-definition. They are reluctant to define specific personal goals and are threatened by the alteration of comfortable routines and the new responsibilities that success inevitably brings. They are dependent people who *require* failure in order to succeed in gratifying their needs to be taken care of by others. The aggressive establishment of boundaries, limits, and tangible achievements which define the self undermines their need to be endlessly "flexible." They want to avoid conflict with anyone over irreconcilable limits.

For all of us, growth inevitably involves "growing pains." The only way around this is not to grow, and work-phobic people have a strong unconscious desire for precisely that kind of safe stagnation. Successful work makes psychological growth visible. The acquisition of productive skills and the clear demonstration of expanding achievement broadcast to others that one is available to be depended on, and that continued wishes to depend on others are no longer appropriate. A work-inhibited person assiduously avoids sending out that message.

Fear of success may manifest itself at various points in the work process. Some people may be great conceptualizers and initiators, and are able to go out on a limb, but they cannot sustain it, and they become paralyzed when they approach achievement. Tangible accomplishment identifies them too sharply as discrete, separate individuals and makes them feel vulnerable.

Other people who fear the spotlight of completed achievement may get lost in the middle phase of work. They are forever reworking something, never letting it go to completion. They feel the need to polish something endlessly, to get *all* the wrinkles out. But their perfectionism is a cover for the fear of letting go and taking on the responsibilities of their achievement. They are also afraid that their success might threaten others, that it might bite a hand that could potentially feed them.

The familiar story of the person who becomes depressed upon assuming chairmanship of the board illustrates the needs of many people who thrive on the support, encouragement, and "nurturing" they get on their way to the top. Once they get there, the pats on the back stop abruptly. Someone else is getting assistance and advice. The "chairman" is now only giving it.

There are some people whose lives seem to lack direction, who either lack definite goals, lack the determination to pursue their goals, or confuse themselves with too many conflicting goals. This group may be extremely work-oriented, but they may never achieve anything of significance or build on what achievements they do realize. They are going in too many directions at once.

It may be the process of work itself, and not only the threat of achievement, that frightens many people with "separation anxiety." The act of concentrating is extraordinarily isolating. Many people can sustain it for only short bursts of time before they experience a sense of disconnectedness. One man confessed that even in his substantial leisure time, he could never read a long novel because of the prolonged concentration it required. He liked poetry, which he could enjoy quickly, or short stories. He always had to keep his office door open when he was alone in it, and even then he felt compelled to make frequent trips to the water cooler, the men's room, or his neighbors' offices, just to "stay in touch."

One of my patients often spoke lovingly about his job. He adored the people in his office, the feel of the plush carpet on his floor, and the gorgeous view of New York Harbor from his fiftieth-floor window. He was fascinated by the wonder of the computer terminal on whose screen data about securities transactions seemed to appear magically. All these elements were part of his *job*, but they were not part of his *work*. His work required that he abstract himself from his surroundings in order to concentrate aggressively on reaching his goals. This he could not successfully do. He enjoyed his *job*, and derived pleasure from it, but he failed at his *work*. With his primary orientation to pleasurable experiences of sensory and emotional fusion and merging, and his merely secondary appetite for satisfaction and achievement, he did not "produce" and was eventually fired from his job.

It is not only the threat of separation from "maternal" nourishment and security which underlies the fear of success in many people. Achievement breeds competitiveness. "Rooting for the underdog" has its origins in the universal unconscious need to deflate the hero, however much we may also worship him. Those people who are afraid of the competitive retaliation of adversaries, and guilty about their own concealed hostilities, will tend to repudiate or disavow success and achievement. They fear criticism and experience it as an attack. In men, early childhood fantasies of castration by an angry or threatened father underlie this dimension of the fear of success.

Little boys will tell you that the part of their selves they fear damage to most is their genitals. The common, even archetypal fantasy of boys and girls is that achievement and mastery are "phallic" qualities, and that the father castrates those who challenge him too much. The Oedipal legend has it that a male child's wish to supplant his father in the bed with his mother resulted in destruction of his eyes, a clear "displacement upward" from the testicles. A friend once amusedly pointed out to me that whenever he went to spank his son for some misdeed, the boy automatically put his hands over his crotch, gladly giving his father full access to his exposed rear end.

Although these early fantasies and complexes are repressed

in childhood, fear of success and achievement in adult men often stems from consciously forgotten but unconsciously lingering fears of retaliation by a powerful, threatening parent from childhood, and to this we give the name "castration anxiety." It is, in actuality, a sort of "commemorative" term, meant to memorialize the source of the anxiety, not to indicate a conscious present-day fear or actual threat.

Geoffrey Phillips, forty-two years old, a floor trader at the New York Stock Exchange, was by his own assessment mediocre at what he did and lacked the necessary drive for success. He looked around at the swarming, feverish activity on the floor of the Exchange and acknowledged the intensely aggressive nature of his business. While other forms of work may be relatively leisurely, the time allotted to reach a specific goal in stock trading may be only seconds. Phillips could complete a multimillion-dollar stock transaction, start to finish, in ten seconds. At the Stock Exchange a split second of inattention may result in failure.

Phillips complained of recurrent September depressions for many years. September was the time he returned to work following his usual August vacations in Virginia. "I can never seem to get myself started," he said. He characteristically complained to his wife that he was "no good, a loser," and her earnest efforts to shore up his confidence always failed. Eventually, by October, he would rouse himself to action, but he never felt successful at what he did. Even when by all external measures he had scored an enormous business triumph, he tended to nullify it by focusing on what he didn't do, or could have done better, rather than what he actually did, and did well.

Everyone liked Geoff Phillips. Extremely handsome, sociable, and well bred, Geoff lived with his charming wife and four children in an elite suburban community outside New York. He attributed what success he had in Wall Street to his sociability. He was well connected, through the "right schools, the right clubs, and the right neighborhood." He knew how to talk to people, to make them feel comfortable. Geoff Phillips epitomized graciousness, and he got a lot of business that way.

He was brought up in a proper Southern Episcopal family. His father was the president of a large Virginia bank, and his mother was a dignified, matronly, but very warm woman whose family had, for generations, been at the top level of Southern aristocracy. Geoff attended a New England boarding school, where he was a mediocre student but a three-letter athlete, and he went on to excel, socially at least, at an Ivy League college. He was a varsity wrestler and president of his fraternity. A continuous refrain from his teachers and his coaches, though, was that he had a lot of potential, but just wouldn't apply himself. He seemed to lack discipline, and when it came to high academic or athletic achievement, he was just not ambitious.

Geoff got his first job directly after college in a large, prestigious brokerage house. Unlike many of his classmates, he did not get an M.B.A. before going into business. This was not the outcome of deliberate, career-oriented calculation on his part. It was, like most other transitions in his life, something that he graciously slided into. The senior partner of his firm, a friend of Geoff's father, had come to dine with the Phillips family one evening, and he offered Geoff a job after his graduation. It was a socially elite firm, and Geoff immediately felt at home there.

When Geoff Phillips felt the need to see a psychiatrist, some twenty-one years later, he had come to the realization that he was temperamentally ill suited for high achievement, at least in today's world. He had been brought up to be a gentlemen, not a success. He had not been aggressive about acquiring special skills from graduate school, and now he felt limited by this. He was surrounded by many people of similar back-ground at the stock exchange, but the most visible and successful traders were "streetwise" men from poor ethnic neighborhoods who had scratched and clawed their way to the top. He equated calculation, strategy, and ulterior attention to defined goals with "scheming" and "deviousness." He refused to accept the idea of aggression in work or at home as a positive, creative drive; he associated it, rather, with surliness and destructive hostility.

Geoff Phillips felt that life's path should be a smooth, uncomplicated flow from day to day. He was bewildered by "complications" in his personal life as well as in his work. At home, he was an extremely loving father and husband. He was able to play endlessly with his children, and the joyousness and general amiability of the Phillips household were immediately visible to anyone. Where Geoff had difficulty was in assuming a disciplinarian role when it was necessary. It was as if he felt too close an identification with his children, and he could not enforce simple rules with any effectiveness.

Although much of Geoffrey Phillips' personality can be attributed to the social mores which governed his upbringing, we cannot stop there in our attempt to understand his overall work inhibition. His story ought to teach us something about the dynamics of ambition and the psychological factors which prevent people from excelling in areas they are fully equipped to master.

Geoff Phillips was the older of two children; his sister was three years his junior. His mother was an effusively warm and doting person who adored her son and lavished love on him. She seemed to have endless patience and tolerance for his "childishness." Unlike many other children in their communi-ty, the Phillips children were not cared for by a series of governesses. Their mother was always available to them, and she saw to it that all other chores were taken care of by her household staff so that she could be a full-time mother. Geoff's father was, in the young boy's eyes, a giant. He was a tough, crafty businessman who wielded awesome power and authority both in the community at large and within his own family.

Neurotic fear stemming from his father's explosive temper played an important role in Geoff's character development and his later problems. His father was never satisfied with Geoff's early successes; he never happily credited his son with praise, but only seemed to emphasize what more he could have done. This seeped into Geoff's unconscious as a feeling that his father was uncomfortable with his son's challenges to him.

Once, in his teens, Geoff and his father won a two-man sailboat race in which Goeff's expertise was clearly recognized by everyone as the decisive element in their victory. His father was livid, and criticized Geoff endlessly for some minor mistakes he had made that may have kept them from setting a record time for the race. What Geoff Phillips came to realize in his therapy was that in order to preserve a relationship with his father, it has been necessary for him never to challenge his father's primacy in the family. His father did not want to be surpassed by his son. The price Geoff had to pay for this was a squelching of his own ambition.

Of course, a great deal of unconscious anger welled up in Geoff throughout his childhood. He denied, at first, having even the slightest feeling of antagonism toward his father, but veiled hints of his frustration did come up in his therapy. In fact, he was sitting on stores of unconscious rage which filled him with great guilt (after all, this was his *father* he was hating), and he punished himself for this by neutralizing his aggressiveness in work, and by discrediting those work achievements he could justifiably have looked at very proudly.

The other major anxiety (after "castration") in Geoff

Phillips' work inhibition was separation anxiety. He was, beneath his handsome, comfortable, self-assured surface, a dependent person. He still yearned for what he had received from his mother in childhood: warm, supportive, sympathetic, automatically available affection and love. He feared the separations and isolation that independent aggressive initiative and achievement would create. He was uneasy with sustained concentration, discipline, and responsibility, because these gave him a feeling of disconnectedness and estrangement. Geoff's sociability and "clubbiness" were, among other things, a cover for his dependency on friendly regard and a sense of belonging to a group which accepted and welcomed him unquestioningly.

His yearly depressions occurred when he was compelled to leave the warm, congenial closeness of the family vacation and return to work. He indirectly appealed to his wife to "baby" him through his depression. The sad fact of his early life is that he was excessively "babied" by his mother as he retreated from his father's awesome presence. His mother protected him (and, perhaps, herself as well) by virtually smothering him. Geoff neurotically looked for and tried to create facsimiles of this closeness in his later life with his wife and even his children.

An interesting example of how Geoff Phillips' two primary neurotic fears coalesced was his virtual terror of public speaking. In his position in the firm, he was called upon frequently to speak before professional and nonprofessional groups about issues relating to the stock market. In his other, more social roles, it was not unusual for him to have to make lengthy toasts or after-dinner remarks at fund-raising affairs. No matter how he tried to talk himself out of this state of mind, he always had the fantasy that his audiences were waiting (as his father would have been) to "chop him up," to mock him for an error, a nervous gesture, or a crack in his voice. At the same time, the exposed isolation of his position also unnerved him. He was out there all alone, all eyes were on him, and he dreaded the recognition (however respectful and admiring it may have been) and the adult responsibility that this represented. Others saw him as a full-fledged man, and this was a fact that he was unconsciously driven to disavow.

Fear of success may also inhibit achievement in people whose parents were men and women of only mediocre accomplishment themselves. Intense guilt over the possibility of showing a father or mother up often prevents their sons and daughters from establishing lofty goals and working aggressively to reach them.

An additional dynamic in fear of success is the fear of loss. The more we succeed, the more we "have," the more we have to lose. Many people who have been traumatized by early-life losses (like the death of a parent or sibling) grow into adulthood believing that they will never be able to hold onto anything of value, and therefore they do not make the effort to acquire it through hard work.

"Fear of failure" has, in my clinical experience, almost always been a rationalized "cover-up" for intense narcissistic competitiveness. Success is basically a relative thing. We all know that no success is ever absolute. There is always someone who has done or will do whatever we have done better. That someone may even be ourselves. Many narcissistic people cannot tolerate the "imperfection" of success, and they deal with this fear by "dropping out" of the competitive struggles of the work world. They berate themselves for any mistakes they may make. They are grudging learners, because accepting someone's teaching implies that there is something they do not know. Being "better" is never good enough for them. They must be the best or nothing. In their all-or-none systems, because nothing is ever "perfect," everything is experienced emotionally as a kind of failure. They are never satisfied. They say that they are afraid of failure, and that this underlies their lack of ambition. But they do not really understand success, or progress toward it when they see it, because of their unrealistic, impatient, perfectionist standards.

There is safety in indolence and procrastination for these people because they can then always say, "I could have done it if I'd only tried harder." Their need to win is so strong that they cannot play, or even look as if they want to play. If they play, they sometimes do very well, but cannot recognize their achievement as anything but failure.

One young woman claimed to be failing "deliberately" throughout her academic career. She "rebelled" against the "values" of her society. She eventually "dropped out," and spent many years wandering aimlessly, criticizing the "rat race" which she had so self-righteously "transcended." This was the only way that her narcissistic needs could come close to being realized.

Finally, some people are unconsciously determined not to succeed because they refuse to give their "selfish" parents any satisfaction for their accomplishments. Parents who emphasized success at all costs for their children often appropriate their children's achievements as their own. The most successful retaliatory weapon these truly rejected children have is to deprive their parents of the trophies they so eagerly sought for themselves through their children.

In women, there are particular dynamics involving the issue of success which may inhibit them in terms of work achievement. Many women feel that no worldly achievement by a female can ever be truly worthwhile, and they therefore stay away from work. Unconscious complexes around the castration theme do often figure into this, but obviously in a very special and quite singular way. They revolve around the much misunderstood concept of "penis envy."

"Penis envy," when it persists after early childhood, is an example of individual neurosis. Like male supremacy or white racism, it is also an expression of cultural neurosis. As I have pointed out before, "neurosis" represents the irrational imposition of infantile fantasies, perceptions, and interpretations of reality on adult experience. To be sure, small children react profoundly to their "misinterpretation" of the clearly perceived anatomical differences between boys and girls. To their way of thinking, the girl is damaged and defective. She lacks something that the boys have—a penis. She is inferior because of it. A common notion is that the little girl has been punished for some misdeed and is therefore permanently marked for her transgression by this castration.

This universal fantasy applies to girls as well as boys. Parents are bombarded with questions about the penis, and children of both sexes show an inordinate amount of curiosity about it, a reflection of its enormous emotional significance. This is not imposed by cultural or environmental training. What *is* culturally determined, however, is the way in which these naturally occurring childhood fantasies are reinforced and made to persist into adulthood, and to seep into various forms of social prejudice.

It is not "objectively" true that a woman is inferior because she has no visible appendage between her legs. It is not "objectively" true that the father's much larger member is synonymous with power and authority. This is only the small child's fantasy, and is typical of a primitive mind's assignment of "causal" significance to facts and situations that are not actually causally related. It is just as "realistic" as the association the small child makes between darkness, nighttime, and danger.

As psychoanalyst Joel Kovel pointed out in his book *White Racism: A Psychohistory*, anti-black prejudice is a kind of cultural neurosis based in part on residues of infantile associations between feces and brown skin. The imposed devaluation of excrement (after its natural *valuation* by the child as a part of his or her body) leads to the automatic devaluation of, and threat by, anything black or dark. "If feces are brown and their skin is brown, then their skin is colored by feces." In the same manner, since the dark of night is threatening to the small child because of its association with the dreaded separation from the parents and the enforced isolation of sleep, darkness and blackness are devalued and feared.

These ideas are the natural fantasies of childhood, but their irrational persistence and incorporation into the conscious or unconscious belief systems of adulthood represent neurosis in an individual or in the society at large. Worldly achievement and expressions of power and authority by women ought not be dismissed or minimized because women, without the penis, are defective or inferior. In terms of objective "adult" reality, one thing has nothing to do with the other. It is only our culture's attachment to infantile fantasied interpretations of anatomical reality which causes us (women as well as men) to diminish the work accomplishments of women. Furthermore, because unconscious fear of their own potential castration persists from infancy into adulthood in many men, women represent a continuous threat. They symbolize the "fact" of castration as a real possibility. For this unconscious reason, women are often not welcome in the phallic work world dominated by men. To "take on" a woman as a wife is one thing, but to have her as a colleague is another. For many men, this leads to a kind of shame by association.

In some women, the unconscious conclusion that the absence of a penis will effectively nullify any concrete personal achievement is a major factor behind their work inhibition. They can only respect or identify with the achievement of men. Only male accomplishment is considered "authentic," and this can often lead to quite self-destructive identifications with male power in the form of masochism and exaggerated submissiveness.

A woman whom I will call Joan Fitzgerald was the oldest of four children, her three younger siblings being boys. When I saw her, she had recently been fired from her job in a legal department of a governmental agency. She was not dismissed for incompetence, but for such things as chronic lateness, inattentiveness to simple directions, and general carelessness.

As a child, she scored in the genius range on IQ tests, and in elementary and high school she was at the top of her class. She received a scholarship to an Ivy League college (with her father's grudging approval, since he felt she should go to work after high school), and it was at college that her performance began to slip below her potential. Everyone who knew her was impressed with her giftedness, but she graduated with a mediocre record. She went on to a good law school, however, where she got through despite doing a minimum of work. She ran around with a nonacademic, local working-class crowd, and had four abortions during her three years at law school. Following graduation, she turned down offers from some highly respected law firms (who could sense her keen intellectual capability despite a poor record) and went to work instead in a routine civil-service job. She was transferred several times because of sloppy, incomplete work, and finally was asked to leave.

Joan came to me with a combination of complaints: failure in work, and a tendency to become involved socially in degrading, self-destructive relationships characterized by indiscriminate, almost compulsive sexuality. At the beginning of our meetings, she disclosed that her dreams were particularly troubling because of their repetitiveness. She said that she had had only two kinds of dreams for many years. The first type she called her "false front" dreams. In these, she would approach a house which she had presumably purchased or belonged to her. It would have a magnificent, impressive facade, but when she went through the entrance, she would realize that it was only a "false front," and the interior would be a shambles—dirty, dingy, and in utter disrepair. Her associations to this recurrent dream imagery led to thoughts about achievement. She felt that any "magnificent accomplishment" (symbolized by the house) she had the capacity to attain would somehow always be inauthentic and a sham, and this was a reason for her lack of motivation to apply her great gifts to work achievement. Why she could not trust that her works would ever be "real" and believable was made clear by her associations to the second type of dream.

These she called her "rape-transformation" dreams. The format of each dream was always the same. She would be walking somewhere and would be accosted by a tall, powerful-looking man. He would expose his "huge" erect penis, both would undress, and he would force her to have intercourse with him. They would then get up, exchange clothing, and walk away. In speaking of the second dream, she revealed her wish, throughout childhood, to be a boy. Although she was the oldest child in the family, her younger brothers got all the respect and admiration for achievement. She was not ignored, but her "successes" were never encouraged or promoted as were those of her brothers. She was praised when she functioned in some capacity as an accessory to male success. Her father spent his own money on his sons' private education, whereas Joan was sent to public school. Her brothers' athletic and worldly accomplishments were applauded by mother and father alike. She was a "tomboy," but her brothers were "real boys."

Through the analysis of her dreams, she came to understand that she was able to feel "whole" only during intercourse, and her fantasy during sex was that she was borrowing the man's penis (symbolized in the exchange of clothing in her dreams) to boost her own self-worth. No substitute, in the form of work accomplishment, would be adequate as a replacement for what she felt was lacking from early childhood. The penis was the difference between her and her brothers, and was the thing, in her neurotic fantasy, which accounted for her parents' valuation of them and devaluation of her. Clearly this oversimplified conclusion did not reflect "objective" truth, but was the result of an unconscious residue from the primitive thinking of early childhood.

Psychoanalyst Annie Reich, in a paper entitled "A Contribution to the Psychoanalysis of Extreme Submissiveness in Women," discussed the case of a woman philosopher who always felt discouraged by her own scholarly efforts until she fell "helplessly" in love with another philosopher through whom she imagined she could achieve "perfection." In the analysis of her *Hörigkeit* (a German term meaning "extreme submissiveness"), it became clear that without a penis, she could never believe in her work. Her continuous yearning for the union of intercourse was the only way to make herself feel complete. She was able, in this way only, to fuse with the penis and the achievements of her philosopher lover.

There is another dynamic in work failure or inhibition that is unique to women. The rivalry between girls and their mothers is a singular one, with a quality that distinguishes it from the rivalry between boys and their fathers. It is a more bitter competitiveness characteristic of that between "have-nots," as opposed to that between "haves." Women are the outsiders in the phallic world of men. They sense their impotence and lack of status (certainly their penis-lessness, as we have seen) quite early in their lives. "Penis envy" is, after all, a metaphor for desire for status in the world, at least the world as it is now.

The rivalry between a woman and her daughter for the husband-father's primary attention can have a virulence that is rarely seen between fathers and sons. It often has the contemptuous quality of sibling competitiviness. A young girl's low self-esteem can be reinforced by the hostility which often comes from her mother. The mother, in her own insecurity, resents "daddy's little girl." She works often to undermine the daughter's self-confidence, and this can lead mightily to a woman's reluctance to dare to succeed in the outside world of occupational achievement.

I have rarely heard, in my experience with male patients, the kind of stories that women tell about the perpetual insults they heard and still hear from their mothers. "That's a nice suit, but your hair is awful." "I'm happy you got the job, but don't you think anyone with half a brain could do that?" When this kind of statement, which of course carries the power of parental authority, reaches the daughter's ears, it has a profound impact on the development of her self-image. After all, "who knows me better than my mother?"

It is easy to see how a woman with occupational aspirations can have three strikes against her chances for success before she starts:

1. She starts out life envying the male penis and status and viewing herself as defective and inferior.
2. Her mother's ambivalence toward her daughter-rival's achievement reinforces the girl's fear of success.
3. Her father and the male-dominated occupational world are reluctant to accept the woman as a full equal.

A man can compete with the like-sex parent and still enjoy the nurturing gifts of his mother. A woman, however, cannot compete with her like-sex parent in so uncomplicated a manner. This sets up a very difficult ambivalence toward the mother, and often prevents the young girl from doing anything which will threaten her mother's fondness for her. What this can lead to is a reluctance to enter and succeed in the work world of men.*

---

*An excellent review of this topic is included in Nancy Friday, *My Mother My Self* (New York: Delacorte, 1977).

PART V

The Crucial Balance

14

Tension and Harmony

The poet Robert Browning said, "Take away love and our earth is a tomb." One hundred years or so later, Albert Camus formulated an equally indisputable truth: "Without work all life goes rotten. But when work is soulless, life stifles and dies." There is no question that the vitality of our lives is a function of our capacities to work and to love. Without satisfying work and pleasurable love, life does become a kind of death. In the course of our growth and maturation, our primitive human instincts of aggression and sex are developed, elaborated, and refined into the heights of working and loving. The quality of our existence depends on the quality of our work and our love.

But, as Santayana pointed out, "Life is not a spectacle or a feast; it is a predicament." The "predicament" has to do not only with fulfilling ourselves in work and in love, but with resolving the inevitable conflict between them. As states of mind, we have seen that they are diametric opposites. Work affirms and defines the self; loving dissolves and obliterates it. Work is structure and order; love is freedom. Work is oriented to the future, to goals; love demands the present. Work is domination and mastery; love is receptivity and submission. Work is mind; love is feeling.

The challenge to develop, balance, and harmonize working and loving is with us every day, regardless of the presence or absence of a job or a loved one. When we establish long-range life goals, when we think about our aspirations in terms of career and family, we are thinking about integrating work and love. We make choices, consciously or unconsciously, about the kinds of people we want to be, by arranging the mix between work and love in our own personalities. Do we become aggressive, creative, productivity-oriented people, or is our personal emphasis on sensitivity, compassion, and leisure? Does the man whose doctor tells him he has one year to live spend that time working feverishly to create something of permanence, or does he abruptly stop work and indulge his pleasures to the fullest?

The graph defined by work on one axis and love on the other offers a means of plotting and categorizing human identities, roles, and occupations. Different fields of endeavor, and individual approaches within those fields, are characterized by different mixtures of work and love. The aggressive, focused, linear, ulteriorized mental set of work applies much more purely to the occupation of an air-traffic controller than to that of a poet. The poet must "love" his materials, he must taste, touch, smell, see, and hear his words with a degree of intimacy that is alien to the person in the control tower but necessary in the creative arts. Recreational activities, like fishing, may be a mixture of work and love; the percentages depend on the particular individual. Some people *need* to catch a fish; others don't. The former are more work- than pleasure-oriented. The latter veer more toward process than product, more toward pleasure than satisfaction, and more toward the immediate present than the future. All of us probably can plot ourselves and our activities somewhere on the following graph.

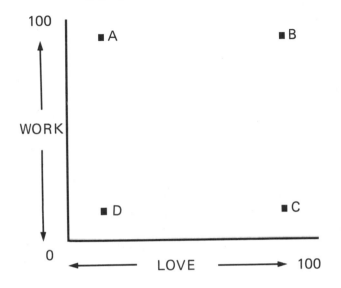

Person A is a work addict, while person C shuns achievement for enjoyment and pleasure. D doesn't fulfill himself on either scale. B is balanced high on both.

Our position on the work-love graph depends on our ability to integrate these conflicting allegiances and develop a personally satisfying balance. The stress over harmonizing these polarities can become especially taxing when demands in one area become particularly strong. Several years ago, it was necessary for me to subordinate my own work goals in order to attend to a family member suffering a prolonged illness. The growth of my practice, and my ability to keep abreast of current professional literature, naturally faltered. By the same token, there have been many times when needs of patients or my own personal desire to extend my competence as a psychiatrist have taken precedence over a particularly important personal or family obligation. Although these kinds of emotional pulls can be powerful and extremely draining, they create a state of dynamic tension that lends vitality and excitement to our lives. For just as work and love conflict with each other, so, paradoxically, do they enrich each other.

The challenge to an individual to find his or her "crucial balance" is always there. Balance can be conceptualized and fostered in several ways. It can be developed within a personality in which the potential to work successfully and to love deeply are harmoniously overlapping and mutually strengthening. This is the most obvious goal, but probably the most difficult to achieve.

Our educational systems play a role in sensitizing people to the need for this kind of ideal balance. Skill-dominated educational approaches turn out more "pure" workers than approaches which also emphasize the experiences of fascination and wonder, and the intrinsic delights of learning. The ideal balance, to elaborate on Eric Berne, is to teach the child which is the jay and which is the sparrow while encouraging him still to look at them and hear them sing.

Another way of thinking about the crucial equilibrium between work and love is to take a long-range longitudinal view. This approach weighs the balances we establish over the course of a life span. There are years when work is the first priority, and years when love takes precedence over achievement. In men, traditionally, the determination to succeed occupationally is consuming through the twenties and thirties, and achievement usually peaks around the forties. It is at this "midlife" phase that men begin to broaden their perspective and address, with greater seriousness than ever before, the loving dimension of their lives. Many men manage to overlook issues of emotional intimacy for long periods because they are so focused on their work achievement. Perhaps they even back into marriage originally as a convenience to their careers only to realize after fifteen years and three children that a loving foundation is absent when they come around to wanting it to be there.

In women, the life-span "graph" may show a dramatically different curve from that of men. The childbearing years have traditionally called for a renunciation of aggressive, mastery-oriented aspirations. Women who take the path of family and children usually adopt the role whose main features are nurturing and empathic qualities, although it is now more and more common for women to attempt to fill occupational and loving roles simultaneously. After children are grown and the day-to-day demands of parenthood are over, mothers who have concentrated exclusively on their home-based loving roles are free to move in the direction of instrumentality, self-affirmation, and aggressive accomplishment. The sad fact, of course, is that while many women are eager to shift priorities in their late thirties and forties, the work world is not necessarily eager to accommodate them without requisite youth, background, and experience.

The "midlife crisis," which psychoanalyst Elliott Jaques first wrote about in 1965 in his paper "Death and the Mid-Life Crisis," is a common phenomenon. It affects most of us in our thirties and forties with the emotional realization of our relative powerlessness to stall or control the passage of time. The more work-oriented the individual and the greater his or her need for mastery, the more difficult and painful this realization is. Perfectionism is no longer viable because the natural effects of time begin to show, and they interfere with perfectionistic machinations. As we get older, our friends begin to die of disease or advanced age. Our own capacities for productivity reach limits, our bodies no longer respond to stresses with the resiliency of youth, and younger people assume positions of authority, often replacing us and sometimes becoming our superiors.

Attitudes toward time and loss vary in midlife and beyond.

Work-addicted people try to deny the inevitable and go on "working" at life till the very end. They fight retirement, refuse to acknowledge the awesome power of time as an adversary, and often become angry, depressed, and even quite paranoid in the face of what they perceive as their decline. Paranoid ideas often enable these people to minimize their sense of personal ineffectiveness and impotence by pointing the finger at "others" who are holding them back. They remain perfectionistic, and they fruitlessly persist in their obsessions with mastery and control. They experience imperfection, Elliott Jaques notes, "as bitter, persecuting failure." They cannot transcend imperfection by accepting it; instead, they feel defeated by it.

Those people who have been able to integrate loving and leisuring attitudes into their lives have a much more serene, healthy sense of resignation about the "getting later" of life. I do not mean by this the resignation of defeat, but the understanding implicit in Francis Bacon's words, "Nature, to be commanded, must be obeyed." I would restate this: "Time, to be mastered, must be obeyed." People capable of leisuring have developed the ability to go "with" things, rather than always feel challenged and "against." They have experienced the pleasure of a "loss" of boundary in intimacy and novelty, and this acceptance of one form of loss prepares them positively for other losses. In this way, we can understand why the French refer to the experience of orgasm as *la petite mort*, "the little death." Those who have truly loved and leisured, and have felt the dissolution of self in the climax of loving, experience a kind of death, a temporary surrender of the self in their fusion with the loved one. They are therefore prepared in a way for the larger death, the death which involves another kind of union—the ultimate union with nature and the return to the earth.

For someone who can tolerate and accept the "coming to the

end" of pleasure, the sense of loss is a small price to pay for the joy which can be derived from the leisuring or loving experience. For Barbara Williams, the lawyer discussed in Chapter 9 whose parents and brother were killed when she was a child, loss was still too immediate and painful. Although she had keen desires for romantic, aesthetic, pleasurable experience, she had to disavow them. She told the following story after coming home from a fall weekend in Vermont, around the time of the colorful changes in foliage:

"The trees were on fire. The colors were so brilliant and varied, I was speechless. I had the desire to 'possess' the beauty of the whole scene, not let it get away from me. If I could only have been Emily Dickinson and been able to drive that beauty, the smoky fragrance, the colors, the light, the cool air, into the framework of a poem. I wanted to have it all to keep and stay just as it was. But even as I was feeling all this beauty, I could also feel it slipping away from me. I was thinking of the fact that I couldn't stand on that hill forever, that it would be night soon, that tomorrow so many of the leaves would have fallen and died."

Barbara perceived artists as aesthetic "dictators" who had the power to incarcerate beauty within the binding frame of a poem or a painting, and keep it from getting away. Knowing that she did not have the skill herself to engage in what she saw as a process of permanent preservation, she shied away from experiences which would excite her in this way. The cost of having to repudiate all experiences of loss ran terribly high for her.

Barbara Williams tried, through psychotherapy, to diminish her consuming emphasis on control. But she had waited too long, and she found herself unable to alter the fixation on her work. She felt, with some justification, that she had nothing to fall back upon, especially no close friendships, and was too frightened to seriously explore alternatives to work.

She was fearful of developing attachments with men because of thoughts like "What if it doesn't work out?" or "What if it works out and he gets sick or dies or falls in love with someone else?" These fears proved to be the undoing of her therapy as well. She would not permit herself to enter into a relaxed "therapeutic alliance" because this could not be a *permanent* relationship. She experienced the pain of eventual termination before she even started. After two months of therapy, she called to say she had decided to stop, and I never heard from her again.

Barbara Williams' story notwithstanding, there are many who are able to shift their emotional priorities to loving and leisuring after the peak of occupational achievement, and a comfortable overall balance to their lives is established. They do not necessarily work with less effectiveness after this midlife point. It is simply that issues of control, mastery, aggressive satisfaction, and accomplishment slide in importance to a position behind those of personal loving intimacy and sensory pleasure. One thirty-eight-year-old financier took a year's sabbatical from the firm he had started at age twenty-six. Seeing an annual growth of about 30 percent take his investors' fund to a value of $110 million had always been "an intoxicating experience" for him. "There was instant gratification. If you did well, you saw it at the end of each day." But, he added, "I never could seem to find a way to substantially reduce my commitment to my work."*

His only way was to impose a strictly enforced year-long sabbatical during which he stayed away from newspapers and ticker tapes, and focused instead on being with his family, visiting tropical-fish stores, taking piano lessons, bottling his own wine, and picking berries for jelly. "At least in some

---

*Reported by Jane Geniesse, "For Financier, a Year's Sabbatical at Home Yields Rewards," *New York Times*, Oct. 1, 1979.

areas, I was richer than before." Mastery had given way to intimacy and sensory experience, and he returned to work with a new and more enlightened perspective.

Many people seek out psychotherapy to assist them through this midlife-crisis period. The process of psychotherapy is largely a process of translation. Its purpose is to interpret habitual behaviors; to translate them into concepts which are emotionally understandable to the patient. We establish a sense of mastery over our *selves* by learning the "language" of our *selves*, of our habitual thoughts, our feelings, and our behavior. In just the same way, we master Chinese by translating it into English. We don't "explain" Chinese, we "translate" it, and once we learn a language, learn to interpret the symbols of that language, we feel stronger and more sure of ourselves in the land where that language is spoken. The "land of our selves" may generate some peculiar "languages," like dentist Richard Chapman's compulsion for work or his interest in pornography, described in chapter 7. Psychoanalytic therapy helped him to translate the alien language of his behavior and gain control over it so that he could expand his emotional horizons into the present instead of living as a victim of his past.

When he first came into psychotherapy, Richard Chapman's sense of self required continuous strengthening and bolstering because of the emotional deprivation which he had experienced early in his life and which left him with needs he still sought to have gratified. Therapy helped him to understand that he no longer really needed the kind of mothering gratification he was so fearful of losing. Gradually, he came to understand that times had changed; instead of building his world only on defending against his vulnerabilities, he could now accept his own strengths.

Psychiatric treatment was a very difficult undertaking for Paul Harrison, the retired real-estate developer with the "smothering" parents, described in chapter 8. He showed a touching kind of courage in agreeing to come to my office for three sessions a week. We agreed that the purpose of the sessions would be not only to treat his acute depression, but to try, through analytic therapy, to prevent it from occurring again in the future. The process was difficult for him on a number of counts. For one thing, *he* was the patient. The very fact that I was someone with a kind of expertise that he lacked, and that exploiting this expertise required his relinquishing some control to me, was a bitter medicine for him to swallow. If therapy was to be successful, I could not be an adversary. The absence of strict "manners" with which to approach our deepening therapeutic relationship was also disconcerting to Paul. He was beset by conflicting, and often embarrassing, feelings, fantasies, and dreams about me which he knew he had to reveal, but which did not jibe with the reality of my position as "the doctor." Furthermore, the format of free association, of saying whatever came to mind without editing or censoring, of coming to sessions without an organized script or specific goals to work toward or a sequence of "topics" which would connect one session to another, was extremely disorienting for Paul. I told him repeatedly that the "topic" was always Paul Harrison, and that this was the fact which would provide us with continuity. But for someone who operated consistently with a linear, goal-oriented mental set, geared only to a sense of mastery and victory, this was far too vague and even frightening a prospect.

The fact that psychotherapy was a process of reflection, translation, and understanding rather than of rigorous scientific explanation, and that insights frequently involved paradoxes rather than simple linear truths, made Paul very uneasy. Often he would refuse to accept the idea that his unconscious mind could be in such stark opposition to his conscious intention. When I first told him that I thought his overwhelming need to control was related to an equally overwhelming unconscious need to be passive and to relinquish control to a powerful maternal figure, he laughed disparagingly. The concept of ambivalence, mutually exclusive feelings about the same person or thing, was very hard for him to grasp.

With all of his resistance to therapy, and, paradoxically, *because* of it, Paul Harrison made great progress. The fuel that makes psychoanalytic therapy go is the "transference neurosis," a term which describes the way that a patient's neurotic problems are transferred to his or her relationship to the therapist. The therapeutic relationship becomes a kind of laboratory. In his behavior and his language with the therapist, the patient repeats, or reexperiences in his fantasies and dreams about the therapist, the nature and scope of the interaction with his mother and father in early life.

The transference neurosis took shape quite rapidly with Paul Harrison. He saw me as a controlling, arbitrary person who pretended to care, but did not really; he thought I was more interested in selfishly pursuing my own professional theories than in allaying his suffering. He was afraid of becoming dependent on me and losing his identity. These fantasies expressed information not about his therapist, but about his parents, whose smothering interaction with him had led powerfully to the formation of his personality. In expressing his feelings about me, he was repeating the attitudes he felt unconsciously toward the parents of his early childhood.

Once Paul Harrison began to come to terms with his ambivalent feelings about his parents' attempts to possess him instead of encouraging his growth, he began to understand his compelling need to see the world only in terms of mastery and victory. Gradually, he became able to perceive others as possible intimates whom he could enjoy, without fearing that they were potentially all-engulfing suppressors of his will and his identity. His compulsion for excelling became moderated to a point where he could enjoy competing when it was appropriate, without feeling driven to impose competition in the realm of personal and love relationships. For the first time, Paul began to understand the concept of true mutuality, and to allow himself the risks of real leisure. As therapy ended, he warmly perceived me as an equal who respected him, not as a performer of extraordinary feats and deals, but as a whole person.

For Virginia Graves, discussed in chapter 5, the woman who spent over twenty years lovingly rearing her children, the midlife shift in emphasis involved a movement toward work and achievement. To attain an overall balance in her life, she had now to focus herself beyond the loving arena of mothering and homemaking. When the last of her children was solidly ensconced in college, she did go to work in an art gallery; several years later, she was able to open her own. She found great pride and a sense of mastery in successfully running her own business. But she felt that there was no way of comparing the gratifications of this experience to the profoundly different ones of the previous twenty years. Each area was unique, and her hope was to be able to attain a harmonious balance between the two. But in terms of being able to define, objectively, a sense of linear personal growth and development, her business clearly succeeded where the mothering role did not. Furthermore, it did substantially diminish her feeling of vulnerability and dependence on her husband. Because her trust in him and, consequently, her feeling of security with him had been permanently altered by his affair, this was a most welcome benefit of her new career. In fact, it probably had a great deal to do with the preservation of their marriage.

The problem for Virginia Graves was not a typical psychiatric one involving deep-seated unconscious needs which were inhibiting her freedom to develop. Rather, it was a kind of "quality of life" dilemma. It involved conscious decisions, which she was free to make psychologically, over the kind of balances she wanted in her life. Ideally, she needed to balance work and love.

According to psychologist David Gutmann, although male and female movement often takes an opposite course along the work-love polarity, men and women ultimately approach each other in what he calls the "normal unisex of later life." Gutmann proposes the interesting theory, based on research demonstrating transcultural regularities in sex-role training, that it is the "chronic emergency" of parenthood which demands the crystallization of specific male and female roles around the vital requirements of young children. He argues that parenthood constitutes "the pivotal stage of the human life cycle, organizing the form and content of the stages which lead up to it, as well as those that succeed it." Fathers need to renounce affiliative impulses if they are to succeed as economic providers, while mothers must suppress their aggressive drives in order to nurture their offspring with greatest effectiveness. In terms of the "crucial balance," this is certainly one pattern of resolution.

Some families show much greater flexibility in role assignments around the "parental emergency" than others, but they are nevertheless able to maintain the necessary balance between nurturing and instrumental qualities. In others, a very rigid, often quite brittle equilibrium is established between an exclusive work role for the man and a narrow caretaking and empathic role for the woman, before and long after the demands of parenthood are present. In this pattern, although a balance of sorts is achieved, it is the most precarious, since it usually represents an unnatural suppression of vital potentiality within each partner.

Let me not give the impression through the foregoing

discussion that the challenge to balance and harmonize the working and loving poles of experience rests solely on people in family groups with children. All people have a stake in this challenge, and each of us must establish his or her own unique personal strategy to meet it.

If people are to make choices in harmonizing love and work at all levels of their lives, they must be as free as they can be to make the "right" choices. By "right," I mean what they truly want, not what they are compelled to choose because of neurotic residues from the past which control their unconscious minds, and not what an "expert" tells them is "right" for them. The role of the psychiatrist is to help to emancipate people from compulsions and blind spots which inhibit their freedom of choice. It is also to help people master the tensions which inevitably arise when choices are made. The Latin root of "decision" is *de-caedere*, "to cut apart." Among other feelings, decision-making always involves the experience of loss. Every time we move in the direction of love or in the direction of work, we are cut off from one alternative; at least temporarily, we lose it. When I am listening to and loving a Duke Ellington tune or sharing experiences with friends, I cannot be reading a book which may help me master an aspect of schizophrenia. When I gain, I lose. This conflict is our predicament, the dynamic tension that underlies the richness and pathos of our lives. Keeping things simple, rigid, and concrete certainly has its rewards, but where there is no struggle and no pain, there is no depth, and little substance.

As our desires for fulfillment in love and work increase, the task of harmonizing and integrating their separate aspects becomes more challenging. No one, of course, has the "truth" about the "correct" resolution of this conflict, psychiatrists included. As Kierkegaard said, "Life can only be understood backward; but it must be lived forward." We proceed, at best, with educated guesses about the optimal compromises for ourselves. But by understanding this predicament, inspecting its sources, and gaining insight into the inner dynamics of work and love, we may be better equipped to approach our own crucial balances.

Bibliography

BOOKS

Alvarez, A. *The Savage God.* New York: Bantam, 1973.

Becker, E. *The Birth and Death of Meaning.* New York: Free Press, 1971.

Bell, D. *The End of Ideology. New York: Free Press, 1960.*

Bergson, H. *Creative Evolution.* New York: Modern Library, 1955.

Black, B. *Principles of Industrial Therapy for the Mentally Ill.* New York: Grune and Stratton, 1970.

Bronowski, J. *The Origins of Knowledge and Imagination.* New Haven: Yale University Press, 1978.

Bruner, J., et al., eds. *Play—Its Role in Development and Evolution.* New York: Basic Books, 1976.

de Grazia, S. *Of Time, Work, and Leisure.* Garden City, N. Y.: Doubleday Anchor Books, 1962.

Federn, P. *Ego Psychology and the Psychoses.* New York: Basic Books, 1952.

Fenichel, O. *The Psychoanalytic Theory of Neurosis.* New York: W. W. Norton, 1945.

Fraiberg, S. *Every Child's Birthright: In Defense of Mothering.* New York: Bantam, 1978.

Frankl, V. *Man's Search for Meaning*. New York: Pocket Books, 1963.

Freeman, L., and Theodore, M. *The Why Report*. Purchase, N. Y.: Arthur Bernhard, 1964.

Freud, S. *Beyond the Pleasure Principle*. New York: Liveright, 1961.

———. *Civilization and Its Discontents*. New York: W. W. Norton, 1961.

———. *Three Essays on the Theory of Sexuality*. New York: Avon, 1962.

Goodman, P. *Growing Up Absurd*. New York: Vintage, 1962.

Haffner, E. *Mothering*. Garden City, N. Y.: Doubleday, 1978.

Hennig, M., and Jardim, A. *The Managerial Woman*. Garden City, N. Y.: Anchor, 1977.

Herrigel, E. *Zen in the Art of Archery*. New York: McGraw-Hill, 1964.

Herzberg, F. *Work and the Nature of Man*. Cleveland: World, 1966.

———, et al. *The Motivation to Work*. New York: Wiley, 1959.

Jaques, E. *Work, Creativity, and Social Justice*. New York: International Universities Press, 1970.

———, and Brown, W. *Glacier Project Papers*. London: Heinemann Educational Books, 1965.

Kernberg, O. *Borderline Conditions and Pathological Narcissism*. New York: Jason Aronson, 1975.

Koestler, A. *The Act of Creation*. New York: Macmillan, 1964.

Kovel, J. *White Racism: A Psychohistory*. New York: Vintage, 1970.

Lakein, A. *How to Get Control of Your Time and Your Life*. New York: New American Library, 1973.

Lasch, C. *The Culture of Narcissism*. New York: W. W. Norton, 1978.

Levinson, D., et al. *The Seasons of a Man's Life*. New York: Knopf, 1978.

Levinson, H. *Executive Stress*. New York: New American Library, 1975.

Lorenz, K. *On Aggression*. New York: Bantam, 1967.

Maccoby, M. *The Gamesman*. New York: Simon and Schuster, 1978.

McLean, A., ed. *Occupational Stress*. Springfield, Ill.: Charles Thomas, 1974.

———, ed. *To Work Is Human*. New York: Macmillan, 1967.

Mills, C. W. *White Collar*. New York: Oxford University Press, 1956.

Nosow, S., and Form, W., eds. *Man, Work, and Society*. New York: Basic Books, 1962.

Oates, W. *Confessions of a Workaholic*. New York: World, 1971.

Ornstein, R. *On the Experience of Time*. New York: Penguin, 1969.

———. *The Psychology of Consciousness*. New York: Harcourt, Brace, Jovanovich, 1977.

Piaget, J. *The Construction of Reality in the Child*. New York: Basic Books, 1954.

———. *The Language and Thought of the Child*. London: Routledge and Kegan Paul, 1948.

Pieper, J. *Leisure: The Basis of Culture*. New York: Random House, 1963.

Reich, A. *Psychoanalytic Contributions*. New York: International Universities Press, 1973.

Roheim, G. *Psychoanalysis and Anthropology*. New York: International Universities Press, 1950.

Rosen, V. *Style, Character, and Language*. New York: Jason Aronson, 1977.

Rosow, J., ed. *The Worker and the Job*. Englewood Cliffs, N. J.: Prentice-Hall, 1974.

Rothman, S. *Woman's Proper Place*. New York: Basic Books, 1979.

Ruddick, S., and Daniels, P. *Working It Out*. New York: Pantheon, 1977.

Salzman, L. *The Obsessive Personality*. New York: Science House, 1968.

Sheehy, G. *Passages*. New York: E. P. Dutton, 1976.

Terkel, S. *Working*. New York: Avon, 1972.

Weber, M. *The Protestant Ethic and the Spirit of Capitalism*. New York: Scribner's, 1958.

Werner, H., and Kaplan, B. *Symbol Formation*. New York: Wiley, 1963.

Whorf, B. *Language, Thought, and Reality*. Cambridge, Mass.: M. I. T. Press, 1956.

Wildenstein, D. *Monet's Years at Giverny*, New York: Metropolitan Museum of Art, 1978.

Work in America. Report of a task force to the Secretary of Health, Education, and Welfare. Cambridge, Mass.: M. I. T. Press, 1973.

ARTICLES

Abraham, K. "Observations on Ferenczi's Paper on 'Sunday Neuroses,'" in R. Fleiss, ed., *The Psychoanalytic Reader*. New York: International Universities Press, 1948.

Bieber, I. "Disorders of the Work Function," in J. Masserman, ed., *Science and Psychoanalysis*, vol. 16 (1970), p. 92.

Black, B., and Chapple, E. "Rehabilitation Through Productive Participation," *Psychiatric Quarterly*, vol. 47, no. 4 (1973).

Block, D. "The Quest for Competence," *Journal of Occupational Medicine*, vol. 19, no. 5 (May 1977), p. 315.

Clifford, R. "Sex as a Chore," *Medical Aspects of Human Sexuality*, April 1979, p. 58.

Cooper, C., and Crump, J. "Prevention and Coping with Occupational Stress," *Journal of Occupational Medicine*, vol. 20, no. 6 (June 1978), p. 420.

Deutscher, M. "Adult Work and Developmental Models," *American Journal of Orthopsychiatry*, vol. 38 (1968), pp. 882–92.

Drellich, M. "The Interrelationships of Work and Play," in J. Masserman, ed., *Science and Psychoanalysis*, vol. 16 (1970), p. 17.

Ekstein, R. "Play and Work," *Journal of Humanist Psychology*, vol. 3 (1963), pp. 20–31.

Engel, M. "Children Who Work and the Concept of Work Style," *Psychiatry*, vol. 30 (1967), pp. 392–404.

Fast, I. "Aspects of Work Style and Work Difficulty in Borderline Personalities," *International Journal of Psychoanalysis*, vol. 56, no. 4 (1975), pp. 397–403.

Fenichel, O. "On the Psychology of Boredom," in *Collected Papers of Otto Fenichel*, vol. 1. London: Routledge and Kegan Paul, 1954.

Freud, A. "Comments on Aggression," *International Journal of Psychoanalysis*, vol. 53, no. 2 (1972), p. 163.

Freud, S. "Formulations Regarding the Two Principles in Mental Functioning," *Collected Papers*, vol. 4. New York: Basic Books, 1959.

———"Instincts and Their Vicissitudes," *Collected Papers*, vol. 4, New York: Basic Books, 1959.

———"Those Wrecked by Success," in "Some Character Types

Met With in Psychoanalytic Work," in *Collected Papers*, vol. 4, New York: Basic Books, 1959.

Furman, E. "Thoughts on Pleasure in Working," *Bulletin of the Philadelphia Psychoanalytic Association*, vol. 19 (1969), pp. 197–212.

Gorney, R. "Work and Love Revisited," *Proceedings of the Fourth World Congress of Psychiatry*, 1966, pp. 2542–44.

Gould, R. "Psychodynamics of Sexual Humor: The Secretary," *Medical Aspects of Human Sexuality*, July 1977, p. 48.

Greenbaum, E., and Greenbaum, H. "Achievers, Losers, and Victims," in J. Masserman, ed., *Science and Psychoanalysis*, vol. 16 (1970), p. 75.

Greenwald, H. "Why Do So Few People Find Work Satisfying?" in L. Freeman and M. Theodore, *The Why Report*. Purchase, N.Y.: Arthur Bernhard, 1964.

Greiff, B. "Psychiatric Consultation at a Graduate Business School," *Psychiatric Annals*, vol. 8, no. 4 (April 1978), p. 27.

Gutmann, D. "Parenthood: A Key to the Comparative Study of the Life Cycle," in N. Datan and L. Ginsberg, *Life Span Developmental Psychology*. New York: Academic Press, 1975.

Guttman, A. "Literature, Sociology, and Our National Game," in Salzman, ed., *Prospects*. New York: Burt Franklin, 1975.

Hatterer, L. "Work Identity," *American Journal of Psychiatry*, vol. 122 (1966), pp. 1284–86.

Heckscher, A., and de Grazia, S., "Executive Leisure," *Harvard Business Review*, July 1959, p. 6.

Hendrick, I. "The Discussion of the 'Instinct to Master,'" *Psychoanalytic Quarterly*, vol. 12 (1943), p. 565.

———. "The Instinct to Master," *Psychoanalytic Quarterly*, vol. 12 (1943), p. 516.

———. "Work and the Pleasure Principle," *Psychoanalytic Quarterly*, vol. 12 (1943), pp. 311–29.

Hess, H. "A Psychiatric Critique of 'Work in America.'" *Journal of Occupational Medicine*, vol. 16, no. 11 (November 1974), p. 736.

———"The Real Peter Principle: Promotion to Pain," in *Stress, Success, and Survival*, Cambridge, Mass.: Harvard Business Review, 1979.

Holmes, D. "A Contribution to the Psychoanalytic Theory of

Work," *Psychoanalytic Study of the Child*, vol. 20 (1965), pp. 384–91.

Jahoda, M. "Notes on Work," in R. Loewenstein, ed., *Psychoanalysis: A General Psychology*, 1966. New York: International Universities Press.

Jaques, E. "Death and the Mid-Life Crisis" and "Disturbances in the Capacity to Work," in *Work, Creativity, and Social Justice*. New York: International Universities Press, 1970.

———. "Note on the Etymology of Work," in *Glacier Project Papers*. London: Heinemann Educational Books, 1965.

Jones, E. "The Theory of Symbolism," in *Papers on Psychoanalysis*. London: Balliere, Tindall, and Cox, 1948.

Kahn, R. "On the Meaning of Work," *Journal of Occupational Medicine*, vol. 16, no. 11 (1974), pp. 716–19.

Kets de Vries, M. "Defective Adaptation to Work," *Bulletin of the Menninger Clinic*, vol. 42, no. 1 (1978), pp. 35–50.

Klein, M. "On the Importance of Symbol Formation in the Development of the Ego," in *Contributions to Psychoanalysis*. London: Hogarth Press, 1948.

Kotulak, R. "Anybody Here Seen a Work Addict?" *Chicago Tribune Magazine*, Dec. 31, 1972, p. 14.

Kramer, Y. "Work Compulsion—A Psychoanalytic Study," *Psychoanalytic Quarterly*, vol. 46 (1977), p. 361.

Lamb, C. "The Sanity of True Genius," *The Works of Charles Lamb*. London: Newnes and Co.

Lantos, B. "Metapsychological Considerations on the Concept of Work," *International Journal of Psychoanalysis*, vol. 33 (1952), p. 439.

———. "Work and the Instincts," *International Journal of Psychoanalysis*, vol. 24 (1943), pp. 114–19.

Lepper, M., and Greene, D. "Turning Play into Work," *Journal of Personality and Social Psychology*, vol. 31, no. 3 (1975), pp. 479–86.

Levi, L. "Occupational Mental Health: Its Monitoring, Protection, and Promotion," *Journal of Occupational Medicine*, vol. 21, no. 1 (January 1979), p. 26.

Machlowitz, M. "Workaholics," *Across the Board*, vol. 14, no. 10 (October 1977), pp. 30–37.

McLean, A., ed., "A Reassessment of Work in America," *Journal of Occupational Medicine*, vol. 16, no. 11 (November 1974).

McMurry, R. "Power and the Ambitious Executive," in *Stress*,

Success, and Survival. Cambridge, Mass.: Harvard Business Review, 1979.

Menninger, K. "Work as a Sublimation," *Bulletin of the Menninger Clinic,* vol. 6 (1942), pp. 170–82.

Menninger, W. C. "Characterologic and Symptomatic Expressions Related to the Anal Phase of Psychosexual Development," *Psychoanalytic Quarterly,* vol. 12 (1943), pp. 161–93.

Munter, P. "Occupational Psychiatry," *Psychiatric Annals,* vol. 8, no. 4 (April 1978), p. 38.

Nadelson, T., and Eisenberg, L. "The Successful Professional Woman: On Being Married to One," *American Journal of Psychiatry,* vol. 134, no. 10 (October 1977), pp. 1071–76.

Neff, W. "Psychoanalytic Conceptions of the Meaning of Work," *Psychiatry,* vol. 28 (1965), p. 324.

Neugarten, B. "Time, Age, and the Life Cycle," *American Journal of Psychiatry,* vol. 136, no. 7 (July 1979), p. 887.

Notman, M. "Midlife Concerns of Women," *American Journal of Psychiatry,* vol. 136, no. 10 (October 1979), p. 1270.

Oberndorf, C. "The Psychopathology of Work," *Bulletin of the Menninger Clinic,* vol. 15 (1951), pp. 77–84.

Pederson-Krag, G. "Women's Work," in L. Freeman and M. Theodore, *The Why Report.* Purchase, N. Y.: Arthur Bernhard, 1964.

Reich, A. "A Contribution to the Psychoanalysis of Extreme Submissiveness in Women," *Psychoanalytic Quarterly,* vol. 9, pp. 470–80.

Reik, T. "Why Work?" in L. Freeman and M. Theodore, *The Why Report.* Purchase, N. Y.: Arthur Bernhard, 1964.

Reisman, D. "The Themes of Work and Play in Freud's Thought," *Psychiatry,* vol. 13 (1950), pp. 1–17.

Renshaw, J. "An Exploration of the Dynamics of the Overlapping Worlds of Work and Family, *Family Process,* vol. 15, no. 1 (1976), pp. 143–65.

Roheim, G. "Psychoanalysis of Primitive Types," *International Journal of Psychoanalysis,* vol. 13 (1932), pp. 2–224.

Rosenthal, S. "Expression of the Emotions in the World of Work," *Psychiatric Opinion,* vol. 15, no. 12 (December 1978), p. 24.

Sacks, M. "A Psychodynamic Overview of Sport," *Psychiatric*

Annals, vol. 9, no. 3 (March 1979), p. 13.

Schwed, H. "Middle Life Crisis and Industrial Workers," *Journal of Occupational Medicine*, vol. 21, no. 1 (November 1979), p. 737.

Segal, H. "Notes on Symbol Formation," *International Journal of Psychoanalysis*, vol. 30, 1957.

Slavson, S. "Aggression," in L. Freeman and M. Theodore, *The Why Report*. Purchase, N. Y.: Arthur Bernhard, 1964.

Steinem, G. "Why Do Women Work, Dear God, Why Do They Work?" *MS.*, vol. 7, no. 9 (March 1979), p. 45.

Storr, A. "The Psychodynamics of Creativity," *Creative Psychiatry*, no. 9, 1977.

Summer, C. "The Managerial Mind," *Harvard Business Review*, July 1959, pp. 69–79.

Thomas, C., moderator. "Sex-Related Problems in Business: A Round-table Discussion," *Medical Aspects of Human Sexuality*, January 1978, p. 60.

Tilgher, A. "Work Through the Ages," in S. Nosow and W. Form, eds., *Man, Work, and Society*. New York: Basic Books, 1962.

Yankelovich, D. "The Meaning of Work," in J. Rosow, ed., *The Worker and the Job*. Englewood Cliffs, N. J.: Prentice-Hall, 1974.

Zaleznik, A. "Management of Disappointment," in *Stress, Success, and Survival*, Cambridge, Mass.: Harvard Business Review, 1979.

Zaleznik, A., and Kets de Vries, M. "What Makes Entrepreneurs Entrepreneurial?" *Business and Society Review*, no. 17, Spring 1976.

About the Author

Jay B. Rohrlich, M.D., is a psychiatrist in private practice in the Wall Street community. His longtime interest in the psychology of working has involved him in organizations such as the American Occupational Medical Association, the Occupational Psychiatry Group, and the Committee on Occupational Medicine of the New York County Medical Society. He is a clinical consultant to many business corporations and financial institutions. He is certified by the American Board of Psychiatry and Neurology and is an active teacher and clinician at the Cornell University Medical College and the New York Hospital, where he is Assistant Clinical Professor and Attending Psychiatrist.